REMEMBER
PEARL
HARBOR!

☆ This Book Belongs To ☆

In late April 1940, the Fleet while anchored in Pearl Harbor put on a spectacular search-light display at night to celebrate the completion of operations in the Pacific for realistic training under battle conditions. Two weeks later they were ordered to remain in Hawaiian waters rather than return to the West Coast. President Franklin D. Roosevelt believed the presence of the Fleet in Hawaii would be a deterrent to further Japanese advances in Asia.

USN

LATEST WAR EXTRA

My

PEARL HARBOR

ScrapBook

★1941★

A Nostalgic Collection of Memories

Japanese Torpedo Bomber
Mitsubishi Type 97
"Kate"

Japanese Type
Mitsubishi Type
"Zeke"

Remember Harbor

Created by

BESS TAUBMAN

Written by

**BESS TAUBMAN &
ERNEST ARROYO**

Design

EDWARD L. COX, JR.

MAPMANIA PUBLISHING PHOENIX, ARIZONA U.S.A.

PUBLISHED BY

MAPMANIA PUBLISHING
Phoenix, Arizona U.S.A.

Printed in China

mypearlharborscrapbook.com

oto: The burning USS *West Virginia* lies sunk in
Pearl Harbor next to the damaged USS *Tennessee*.

Photo: Japanese torpedo and dive bombers strike
.S. Fleet at their berth at Ford Island.

-IN-PUBLICATION

algic collection of memories /
Taubman & Ernest Arroyo ;
design by Edward L. Cox, Jr. — 1st ed.
p. cm.
Includes bibliographical references.
SUMMARY: A re-created World War II nostalgic-style scrapbook details
Japan's attack on Pearl Harbor, Hawaii, December 7, 1941, and its
repercussions, integrating authentic photographs, newspaper clippings,
maps, telegrams, and a multitude of vintage artifacts.
LCCN 2013908620
ISBN-13: 978-1-883443-07-8
ISBN-10: 1-883443-07-5

1. Pearl Harbor (Hawaii), Attack on, 1941—Pictorial works.
I. Arroyo, Ernest. II. Title.

D767.92.T38 2013   940.54'26693
QBI13-600089

★ TERRITORY OF HAWAII ★

Handwritten note:

Greetings!

Victoria Sutherland
suggested I include a
note on this LOC page.
Book was printed in
December 2013, yet
has a 2014 Copyright.
She OK'd book for
entry.
Thanks so much!!
Enjoy!, Bess Taubman

To Philip, Mariann & David Altfeld, my loving parents and brother whose unconditional love, extraordinary support and always being there makes everything possible. B.T.

To my children Soda, Daysia, Ava, Levi, Hazel and my beautiful wife Nikki. E.C.

Dedicated in loving memory of my mother Yetta. E.A.

Table of Contents

Foreword
Commemoration

Part I

Peacetime Hawaii . . . . Preface
War! Newspapers December 7th 1941 1
War Declared on Japan by U.S. 3

Part II

Prelude to War 5
Japan's Blueprint 7
Breakdown in Diplomacy 9
U.S. Leaders of Defense / Japanese Leaders of War . . . 11
Timeline: 1941 13
Hawaii Operation 15
Kido Butai 17
Tora! Tora! Tora! 19
"Jake" Sea Plane 21
"Val" Dive Bomber 22
"Kate" Torpedo / High Level Bomber 23
"Zero" Carrier-Based Fighter 24
Japanese Midget Secret Subs 25

Part III

Battleship Row 27
Devastation at Pearl Harbor 29
American & Japanese Losses 35
Warning Radar? 37
Pride of the Pacific Fleet 39
U.S. Planes at Pearl Harbor 41

Part IV

USS *Arizona* Destroyed 43
USS *California* 45
USS *Maryland* 47
USS *Nevada* 49
USS *Oklahoma* 51
USS *Pennsylvania* 53
USS *Tennessee* 55
USS *West Virginia* 57
USS *Utah* 59

Part V

Pearl Harbor Posters 61
Years That Followed 63
Japanese Internment 65
On The Home Front 67
Rationing in World War II 69
Uncle Sam Wants You! 71

The sprawling Pearl Harbor Navy Base as it looked in May, 1940. Bordering on the bottom left of Ford Island (center) is Battleship Row. Across the channel are the yard repair shops, dry docks, sub base and tank farms. Near the harbor entrance (top left of Ford Island) is the Army Air Base, Hickam Field. Seen moored in East Loch (bottom right) is a large group of cruisers and destroyers of the Fleet.

FOREWORD by

DANIEL MARTINEZ
National Park Service Chief Historian
WW II Valor in the Pacific National Monument at Pearl Harbor

Scrapbooks have been part of the human experience since the early 1500's. In England the early scrapbooks began with the gathering of recipes, sketches and letters. As the centuries passed the collecting of personal memories became more refined in the late 1800's with the introduction of photographs, newspaper and magazine clippings. Scrapbooking in the United States saw its greatest increase during years of the Second World War. It was a way that cherished memories were kept, shared and treasured during one of the most difficult experiences of a nation and its citizens engulfed in World War II.

My Pearl Harbor Scrapbook 1941 is an imaginative publication that uses the scrapbook format to communicate the visual and tactile experience of what happened on that day... December 7, 1941.

Bess Taubman with Ernest Arroyo and Edward L. Cox Jr. have re-created through artifacts, photos, illustrations, maps and clippings a scrapbook that conveys the history and spirit of the attack on Oahu and Pearl Harbor. This unique collection of original and recreated materials will provide a literary encounter that will enrich the reader's knowledge about the day. It was a day that changed the lives of all Americans that lived then and those that live now.

The design of the scrapbook by Bess Taubman and graphic designer, Edward L. Cox, Jr. is simply remarkable. Their integration of images such as clippings, charts, drawings and pictures bring back the feel and look of a 1941 scrapbook. As a historian I appreciate and treasure innovative ways to convey history in a manner that insures an educational journey.

Today, a national memorial rests over the remains of a sunken battleship in Pearl Harbor. Over 900 sailors, Marines and officers are entombed within the ship. Oil still escapes from the ship in small portions every few minutes. The USS *Arizona* Memorial reaches out to those who come to honor the dead and to those who embrace the premise of reconciliation that is central to the Memorial's theme of peace and harmony.

So as you begin your journey into time through the pages of *My Pearl Harbor Scrapbook 1941* keep in mind that at the end of your literary road is the realization that this war happened to real people, both young and old.

Commemoration

"They fought together as brothers in arms; they died together and now they sleep side by side...To them, we have a solemn obligation — the obligation to ensure that their sacrifice will help make this a better and safer world in which to live."

Fleet Admiral Chester William Nimitz
Commander in Chief of Pacific Forces
for the United States during World War II

On September 2, 1945, after accepting
the official surrender of Japan in Tokyo Bay.

Kau Kau Corner

A 24-hour drive-in located on the busy corners of Kalakaua Avenue and Kapiolani Blvd. in Honolulu.

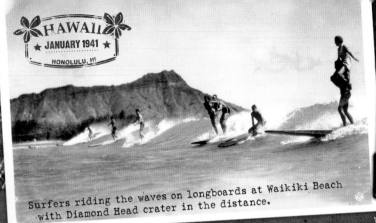

Surfers riding the waves on longboards at Waikiki Beach with Diamond Head crater in the distance.

S. S. Lurline

The Aloha Tower stands as a warm "aloha" welcome to all who arrive in Honolulu by ship.

The Territory of Hawaii's breezy tropical climate and warm blue ocean beckoned visitors with the mystique of idyllic island life. Luxury ocean liners and Pan Am's Clipper began bringing tourists to Honolulu in the mid-1930's. Passengers were greeted by the distinctive sight of the Aloha Tower, lei makers and the lush green hills of the Wai'anae and Koo'lau mountains. Even the first commercial aloha shirts made their appearance in 1936. Island life seemed ideal.

But in the summer of 1940, the Pacific Fleet was moved from California to Pearl Harbor as a way to intimidate Japan's aggressive actions. Yet so far away from the rest of the world in the middle of the Pacific Ocean, life in Hawaii seemed untouched, despite mandatory practice evacuations and blackout drills. On the horizon, foreboding clouds gathered over Asia and slowly drifted towards the Islands that would change this way of life forever.

MAY, 1940

After training exercises, the Pacific Fleet anchors at Pearl Harbor for liberty and "R & R."

December 6, 1941

Jack Miller Frank Kosa Clifford Olds

HULA DANCING

Hula in the park was commonplace as culture began to shift towards entertainment and tourism. Performances of Hawaiian music as well as hula became synonymous with the magic of the "aloha" spirit.

Olds was aboard the USS WEST VIRGINIA when it was sunk. He was trapped inside a sealed compartment until December 23. He did not survive.

Peace Time Hawaii 1941 *Preface*

Moonlight in Waikiki over Diamond Head.

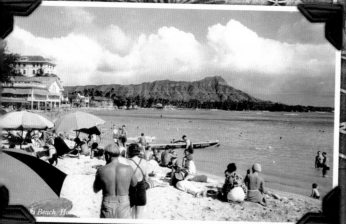
Beautiful Waikiki Beach with its white sand and tropical blue waters was a haven for all who came to visit.

A group of sailors on liberty in Honolulu enjoy a round of Primo Beer at the Kiwali Inn.

HAWAIIAN GIRL ON CANNON
On Army Day a young girl poses on a cannon displayed at the Iolani Palace grounds. This cannon had just won the prize for "top field" gun.

DANGER AIR BRAKES

The legendary Royal Hawaiian Hotel in Waikiki, affectionately known as the Pink Palace of the Pacific, was closed to tourists during the war and was taken over by the Navy.

U.S.S. UTAH

PLAN OF THE DAY FOR SUNDAY
the 14th of SEPT., 1941.

Duty Head of Department - Lt.Comdr.
CPO Duty Section - FIRST.
Duty Watch - STARBOARD.
Uniform of the Day - UNDRESS BLUES.
Duty Boat Crew No. 2; Standby No. 3

ROUTINE - Port, Sea.

0530 Reveille.
0730 Breakfast.
0800 Muster on stations, make report
      Hoist all boats, rig in gangway
      preparations for getting underw
      in M.W.B. to wait for him. Hoi
0830 Sick Call.
0930 Station regular and special sea
0945 All departments be ready to get
1000 Underway.
1200 Dinner.
1730 Supper.
1930 Movies.
2100 Pipe down.

PLAN OF THE DAY FOR
the 15th of SEPT.

ROUTINE - Sea.

0530 Call all Idlers.
0500 Turn to. Wash down.
0645 Up all hammocks.
0700 Air Bedding.
0730 Breakfast.
0800 Quarters for muster and physical dr
0815 Turn to. Gunnery drill.
0830 Sick Call.
1130 Messcooks inspection.
1200 Dinner.
1300 Turn to. Continue ship's work, Gunn
1600 Emergency drill.
1730 Supper.
1930 Movies.
2100 Pipe down.

MOVIE TITLE FOR SATURDAY: "PARTIES IN CRIME
Roscoe Karns, and Muriel Hutchinson. (PARA.
MOVIE TITLE FOR SUNDAY: Short: "FISHING FEVE
Feature: "A SHOT IN THE DARK" with Ricardo C
Ken Wynn, and Regis Toomey. (VITA. 6 reels

Honolulu Star-Bulletin 1st EXTRA

8 PAGES—HONOLULU, TERRITORY OF HAWAII, U. S. A., SUNDAY, DECEMBER 7, 1941—8 PAGES • PRICE FIVE CENTS

WAR !

OAHU BOMBED BY JAPANESE PLANES

(Associated Press by Transpacific Telephone)

SAN FRANCISCO, Dec. 7.—President Roosevelt announced this morning that Japanese planes had attacked Manila and Pearl Harbor.

SIX KNOWN DEAD, 21 INJURED, AT EMERGENCY HOSPITAL

Attack Made On Island's Defense Areas

By UNITED PRESS
WASHINGTON, Dec. 7.—Text of a White House announcement detailing the attack on the Hawaiian islands is:

CIVILIANS ORDERED OFF STREETS

The army has ordered that all civilians stay off the streets and highways and not use telephones.

Evidence that the Japanese attack has registered some hits was shown by three billowing pillars of smoke in the Pearl Harbor and Hickam field areas.

All navy personnel and civilian defense workers, with the exception of women, have been ordered to duty at Pearl Harbor.

The Pearl Harbor highway was immediately

ANTIAIRCRAFT GUNS IN ACTION

First indication of the raid came shortly before 8 this morning when antiaircraft guns around Pearl Habor began sending up a thunderous barrage.

At the same time a vast cloud of black smoke arose from the naval base and also from Hickam field where flames could be seen.

BOMB NEAR GOVERNOR'S MANSION

Shortly before 9:30 a bomb fell near Washington Place, the residence of the governor.

Hundreds See City Bombed

Hundreds of Honolulans who hurried to the top of Punchbowl soon after hostilities began to fall, saw spread out before them the whole panorama of surprise attack and defense.

Names of Dead and Injured

CITY IN UPROAR

Within 10 minutes the city was in an uproar. As bombs fell in many parts of the city, and in defense areas the defenders of the islands went into quick action.

Army

The attack centered in the Pearl Harbor, Army authorities said:

"The rising sun was seen on the wing tips of the airplanes."

Although martial law has not been declared officially, the city of Honolulu was operating under M-Day conditions.

Governor Poindexter urged all residents of Honolulu to remain off the street, and the people of the territory to remain calm.

Mr. Doty reported that all major disaster council wardens and medical units were on duty within a half hour of the time the alarm was given.

Workers employed at Pearl Harbor were ordered at 10:10 a. m. not to report at Pearl

HAWAII MEETS THE CRISIS

Honolulu and Hawaii will meet the emergency of war today as Honolulu and Hawaii have met emergencies in the past—swiftly, calmly and with immediate and complete support of the officials, officers and troops who are in charge.

Governor Poindexter and the army and navy leaders have called upon the public to remain calm; for civilians who have no essential business on the streets to stay off, and for every man and woman to do his duty.

That request, coupled with the measures promptly taken to meet the situation that has suddenly and terribly devel-

---

At 7:55 a.m. Sunday morning, December 7, 1941, Japanese planes began bombing Pearl Harbor, Hawaii in a surprise attack against the United States. Word was spreading like wildfire in Honolulu and competing newspapers rushed to get the shocking story out. A record 250,000 copies of the Honolulu Star-Bulletin newspaper in 3 special editions—known as Extras—became one of America's most historic front pages of all time.

Many copies and reproductions of the famous Honolulu Star-Bulletin front pages have been duplicated over the years. The authentic version of the paper's 1st Edition displays two inadvertent ink smudges. One in the top headline and another between the letters "A" and "R" in WAR. These press mark smudges identify the authentic versus the fake.

WAR EXTRA

BALTIMORE THE NEWS-POST

The Largest Evening Circulation in the Entire South

VOL. CXL—NO. 28   MONDAY, DECEMBER 8, 1941   PRICE 3 CENT

JAPS BOMB U. S. ISLANDS

Honolulu Star-Bulletin 2nd EXT

8 PAGES—HONOLULU, TERRITORY OF HAWAII, U. S. A., SUNDAY, DECEMBER 7, 1941—8 PAGES   ★★★ PRI

DEATHS OVER 400 ON OAHU, LATEST REPOR

ANNOUNCES "STATE OF WAR" WITH U

Raids On Guam, Panama Are Repor

ackout Tonight; Fleet Here Moves Out to

Four Waves, Start At 7:55, Oahu Hit **Governor Proclaims National Emergency**

Pearl Harbor
1941

In the late 1930's, the protected harbor of Pearl Harbor, Hawaii was home to an active base for the repair and refueling of U.S. Navy ships when on maneuvers. It was also an exotic liberty port for sailors on shore leave. As diplomatic relations began to deteriorate in the 1940's between the United States and Japan, President Roosevelt as Commander in Chief ordered the Pacific Fleet to be permanently based at Pearl Harbor as a deterrent to Japanese threats in the Far East. The Pacific Fleet was comprised of nearly two hundred ships that included nine gallant battleships.

One of Japan's main objectives was to destroy or severely weaken the U.S. Pacific Fleet at Pearl Harbor, thereby keeping the U.S. from interfering with Japan's ongoing plans for the conquest and occupation of Southeast Asia. The Japanese Navy had developed the power of aircraft carrier warfare as a new strategy to spearhead the attack. From that moment forward the world would be changed forever.

On December 7, 1941, there were no U.S. carriers in port. The seven giant battleships moored on the South shore of Ford Island, known as Battleship Row, became the prime target and bore the brunt of the attack. As a result, the USS *Arizona, California, Oklahoma* and *West Virginia* were sunk. The USS *Nevada* was beached off Hospital Point and sank later when moved to Waipio Point. Of the twenty-one ships either sunk or damaged at Pearl Harbor only three never returned to active service. A total of 164 Army and Navy planes were destroyed and another 159 were damaged but later repaired.

Within 15 minutes, the ships at Battleship Row had been wiped out. 1,177 officers and crewmen perished almost instantly when the *Arizona* took a direct hit and exploded from a single 1,760 lb. bomb that struck the forward ammunition storage area three decks below. When the last Japanese planes had returned to their carriers, the crippling impact of the surprise attack left nearly 2,400 American military and civilian casualties in its wake.

Honolulu Star-Bulletin

1ST EDITION — TWO SECTIONS

24 PAGES—HONOLULU, TERRITORY OF HAWAII, U. S. A., MONDAY, DECEMBER 8, 1941—24 PAGES · *Save this!* · ★★★ PRICE FIVE CENTS

MONDAY, DECEMBER

WAR DECLARED ON JAPAN BY U.S.

The surprise attack on the U.S. Pacific Fleet in Pearl Harbor on December 7th, 1941 changed the world. On December 8th, America was ready to fight back. President Roosevelt appealed to Congress to declare war against Japan. In one of the most famous speeches of the 20th century, Roosevelt spoke for six and a half minutes to a shocked and outraged nation glued to their radios. He ended with "I ask that the Congress declare that since the unprovoked and dastardly attack by Japan on Sunday, December seventh, a state of war has existed between the United States and the Japanese Empire."

TELEGRAM

"AIR RAID PEARL HARBOR...THIS IS NOT DRILL"

...WERE THE WORDS THAT RESONATED THROUGHOUT PEARL HARBOR AND AROUND

THE WORLD ON DECEMBER 7, 1941... HAWAII WAS "DELIBERATELY ATTACKED."

LOSSES WERE GRAVE... THE AFTERMATH, SHOCKING.

1941 DEC 8 PM 12:30

③ THE FASTEST WAY TO SEND MESSAGES IS BY TELEGRAPH OR CABLE

Congress voted 388-1 for Declaration of War against Japan! It was pacifist first elected woman to Congress, Jeannette Rankin from Montana, who was the only "No" vote against war.

(Photos: above left and right)

December 8, 1941-- President Franklin D. Roosevelt addressed the nation day after the attack on Pearl Harbor and asked Congress for a Declaration of War against the Empire of Japan

ROOSEVELT

DRAFT No. 1

December 7, 1941.

PROPOSED MESSAGE TO THE CONGRESS

Yesterday, December 7, 1941, a date which will live in ~~world history~~ infamy

the United States of America was ~~simultaneously~~ suddenly and deliberately attacked

by naval and air forces of the Empire of Japan.

The United States was at the moment at peace with that nation and was ~~continuing the~~ still in conversation with its Government and its Emperor looking

toward the maintenance of peace in the Pacific. Indeed, one hour after

Japanese air squadrons had commenced bombing in Oahu ~~Hawaii and the Phili~~

the Japanese Ambassador to the United States and his colleague deli

to the Secretary of State a formal reply to a ~~former~~ recent American message from the

~~Secretary.~~ This reply ~~contained a statement~~ stated that it seemed useless that diplomatic negotiations

~~must be considered at an end, but~~ it contained no threat ~~and no~~ or hint of ~~an~~ war or

armed attack.

It will distance ~~of Manila, and especially~~ of

Hawaii from Japan ~~obvious~~ that ~~the~~ attack ~~were~~ was deliberately

planned many days or even weeks ago. During the intervening time the Japanese Govern-

ment has deliberately sought to deceive the United States by fal

statements and expressions of hope for continued peace.

"It was just the kind of unexpected thing the Japanese would do. At the very time they were discussing peace in the Pacific, they were plotting to overthrow it"

— President Franklin Delano Roosevelt

ROOSEVELT'S INFAMY SPEECH

"Yesterday, December 7th, 1941 -- a date which will live in infamy -- the United States of America was suddenly and deliberately attacked by naval and air forces of the Empire of Japan....

...The attack yesterday on the Hawaiian islands has caused severe damage to American naval and military forces. I regret to tell you that very many American lives have been lost. In addition, American ships have been reported torpedoed on the high seas between San Francisco and Honolulu..."

DEMOCRATIC NOMINEE 1940

WASHINGTON. D.C. SEP 18 11-AM

UNITED STATES POSTAGE

ROOSEVELT

ROOSEVELT

4125 Road

4

PRELUDE TO WAR

JAPAN'S EXPANSION

WASHINGTON D.C., May 15th.
Tensions between the United States and Japan increased throughout the 1930's. The Japanese believed it was their destiny to rule all of Southeast Asia while the United States struggled to keep this area free from foreign domination. Japan lacked oil reserves, tin and rubber. Its foreign policy revolved around the continued acquisition and control of these and other vital natural resources.

EUROPE COULDN'T DEFEND ITSELF

WASHINGTON D.C., May 15th.
In the mid-1930's America was still recovering from the great Depression. World War II began on September 1, 1939, when Adolf Hitler's Nazi Germany invaded Poland. By 1940 Belgium, Holland and France, quickly fell into German hands. Britain stood alone against the threat of Nazi invasion.

JAPAN DOMINATES SOUTHEAST ASIA

WASHINGTON D.C., May 17th.
Japan quickly realized that Europe was in trouble as Hitler's veil of darkness descended across the continent. They knew that the Western nations were too preoccupied to defend their colonial possessions in Southeast Asia French Indochina, Netherlands East Indies, British Borneo, Burma, Malaya Singapore and Hong Kong. Japan invaded and occupied broad areas of Southeast Asia, pursuing its economic vision to control the territory. Parts o China, the occupied portion of French Indochina and many other territorie fell to Japanese domination. By 1941 Japan signed the Tri-Partite Pact and officially joined Germany an Italy as an ally.

TOP: Victorious troops of the Imperial Japanese Army march into the city of Shanghai.
BOTTOM: Japanese troops take position on burning rooftop in Manchuria.

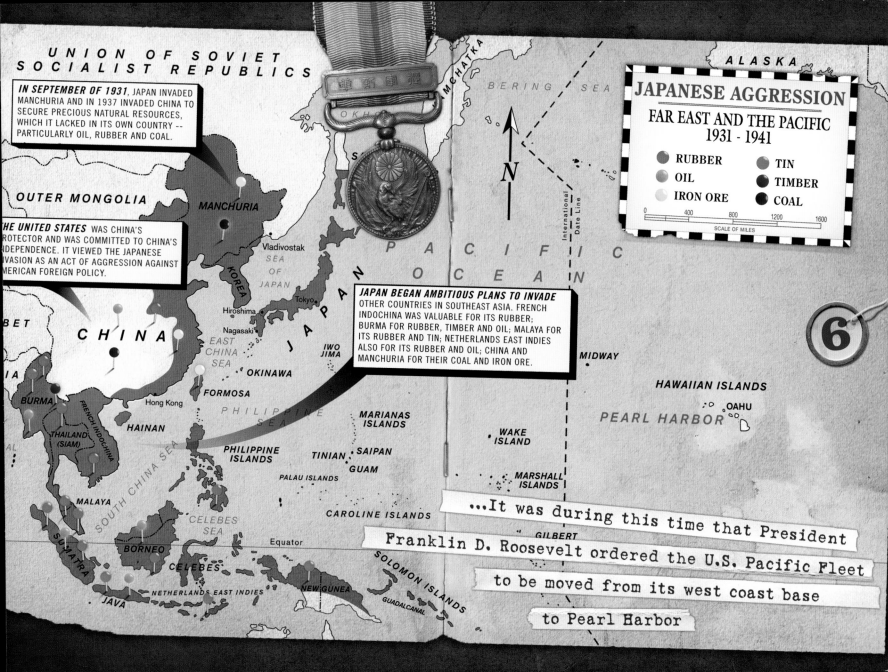

UNION OF SOVIET
SOCIALIST REPUBLICS

IN SEPTEMBER OF 1931, JAPAN INVADED MANCHURIA AND IN 1937 INVADED CHINA TO SECURE PRECIOUS NATURAL RESOURCES, WHICH IT LACKED IN ITS OWN COUNTRY -- PARTICULARLY OIL, RUBBER AND COAL.

OUTER MONGOLIA

THE UNITED STATES WAS CHINA'S PROTECTOR AND WAS COMMITTED TO CHINA'S INDEPENDENCE. IT VIEWED THE JAPANESE INVASION AS AN ACT OF AGGRESSION AGAINST AMERICAN FOREIGN POLICY.

MANCHURIA

KAMCHATKA

BERING SEA

ALASKA

OKHOTSK

N

International Date Line

PACIFIC OCEAN

JAPANESE AGGRESSION
FAR EAST AND THE PACIFIC
1931 - 1941

- RUBBER
- OIL
- IRON ORE
- TIN
- TIMBER
- COAL

0   400   800   1200   1600
SCALE OF MILES

Vladivostak

SEA OF JAPAN

KOREA

CHINA

TIBET

Hiroshima

Nagasaki

Tokyo

JAPAN

IWO JIMA

EAST CHINA SEA

OKINAWA

FORMOSA

Hong Kong

BURMA

FRENCH INDOCHINA

THAILAND (SIAM)

HAINAN

PHILIPPINE SEA

JAPAN BEGAN AMBITIOUS PLANS TO INVADE OTHER COUNTRIES IN SOUTHEAST ASIA. FRENCH INDOCHINA WAS VALUABLE FOR ITS RUBBER; BURMA FOR RUBBER, TIMBER AND OIL; MALAYA FOR ITS RUBBER AND TIN; NETHERLANDS EAST INDIES ALSO FOR ITS RUBBER AND OIL; CHINA AND MANCHURIA FOR THEIR COAL AND IRON ORE.

MIDWAY

HAWAIIAN ISLANDS

PEARL HARBOR   OAHU

MARIANAS ISLANDS

WAKE ISLAND

PHILIPPINE ISLANDS

TINIAN   SAIPAN

GUAM

PALAU ISLANDS

MARSHALL ISLANDS

MALAYA

SOUTH CHINA SEA

CELEBES SEA

CAROLINE ISLANDS

Equator

SUMATRA

BORNEO

CELEBES

NETHERLANDS EAST INDIES

NEW GUINEA

SOLOMON ISLANDS

GUADALCANAL

GILBERT

JAVA

(6)

...It was during this time that President Franklin D. Roosevelt ordered the U.S. Pacific Fleet to be moved from its west coast base to Pearl Harbor

JAPAN'S BLUEPRINT

America's national security in the Far East was jeopardized by Japan's continued aggression in Southeast Asia. The United States reacted strongly by:

- freezing all Japanese assets in the United States.
- establishing an embargo on all trade with Japan.
- suspending all shipments of raw material, oil, scrap metal and high octane gasoline.

TENSIONS BUILD

- The Japanese demanded that the United States remove its trade embargo.
- The United States demanded that Japan remove its troops from China.
- Both nations refused to budge.
- Japan felt it had no choice but to continue its plans to invade Southeast Asia as well as to remain in China.
- While Japan would soon be in a position to control the area's vast natural resources, Japan also recognized that it was moving inevitably towards war with the United States!

JAPAN NEEDED...

- ★ OIL
- ★ TIN
- ★ RUBBER
- ★ CHEMICALS
- ★ MACHINERY
- ★ STEEL
- + other strategic goods

This enemy map was recovered from a downed Japanese aircraft identifying all U.S. ship locations at Pearl Harbor.

Japanese army tanks in a column crossing a river in China, 1939.

A SURPRISE ATTACK

TELEGRAM

U.S. BLOCKS TRADE WITH JAPAN

...UNDER PRESSURE FROM THE U.S. EMBARGO, JAPAN FELT IT HAD NO CHOICE

BUT TO CONTINUE THE INVASION OF SOUTHEAST ASIA AND PLAN

A SURPRISE ATTACK TO NEUTRALIZE THE U.S. PACIFIC

FLEET AT PEARL HARBOR...

1940 SEPT PM 7:32

THE FASTEST WAY TO SEND MESSAGES IS BY TELEGRAPH OR CABLE

Fearing that the U.S. Pacific Fleet would become a formidable obstacle to the Japanese conquest of Southeast Asia, Admiral Isoroku Yamamoto, the Commander in Chief of the Japanese Combined Fleet, visualized a bold attack on the Pacific Fleet at Pearl Harbor.

Although nationalis and militaristic pr was driving Japan tow war with the Uni States, some Japan military leaders w concerned about long-range implicati of a lengthy war with industrial giant.

> **"WE SHOULD DO OUR VERY BEST... TO DECIDE THE FATE OF THE WAR ON THE VERY FIRST DAY."** — *Isoroku Yamamoto*

YAMAMOTO'S APPREHENSION

Of all the Japanese leaders, it was Admiral Yamamoto who resisted the idea of war with America. He felt Japan had no hope of victory against the United States. Educated at Harvard University and later serving as naval attaché in Washington in the 1920's, Yamamoto knew first-hand the industrial might of the United States. He knew America was superior to Japan in technology, science and natural resources. He worried about relations with Germany and mistrusted Japan's involvement in the Tri-Partite Pact, joining Italy, Germany and Japan. Even Admiral Yamamoto expressed doubt and apprehension over Japan's headlong push toward conflict.

Admiral Isoroku Yamamoto
April 4, 1884 – April 18, 1943

> **...SHALL RUN WILD CONSIDERABLY FOR THE FIRST SIX MONTHS OR A YEAR, BUT I HAVE UTTERLY NO CONFIDENCE FOR THE SECOND AND THIRD YEARS."** — *Isoroku Yamamoto*

Yamamoto was also a fierce loyalist, always putting his country first. His idea of delivering a fatal attack on Pearl Harbor utilizing most of Japan's military fleet of aircraft carriers thousands of miles away from home was indeed ambitious. The planning was meticulous and the need for secrecy and surprise was paramount!

Breakdown in Diplomacy...

Washington D.C.

DURING THE SUMMER MONTHS OF 1941, JAPANESE–AMERICAN RELATIONS CONTINUED TO DETERIORATE. THE U.S. INSISTED THAT JAPAN CEASE ALL HOSTILITIES IN CHINA AND WITHDRAW ENTIRELY. JAPAN DID NOT WANT U.S. INTERFERENCE IN CHINA. THEY WANTED TO RESUME TRADE RELATIONS BY LIFTING THE U.S. EMBARGO ON OIL AND OTHER VITAL RAW MATERIALS JAPAN NEEDED.

Each side appeared genuinely anxious to make a peace settlement, but neither would yield to anything the other considered significant.

JAPAN DISPATCHES SPECIAL ENVOY SABURO KURUSU

The Japanese Government had been pressing their Ambassador Kichisaburo Nomura in Washington to reach an early settlement. By late fall impatient Japanese militarists were determined to go to war if final attempts at diplomacy failed. Japan dispatched Special Envoy Saburo Kurusu, an experienced diplomat, with instructions to assist Nomura in bringing negotiations to a favorable conclusion.

Ambassador Nomura greets Special Envoy Saburo Kurusu upon his arrival in Washington.

OCTOBER 1941

U.S. - Japanese Negotiations Continue

In the waning days of November, negotiations reached an impasse. Secretary of State, Cordell Hull responded to Japan's latest proposal of November 27 with America's Ten-Point Memorandum, insisting that Japan give up what it had gained in China and Indo-china. But this was unacceptable to Japan. It would mean a great "loss of face and prestige" in Asia. Tokyo advised Nomura and Kurusu that a deadline of November 29 for reaching a favorable solution "absolutely cannot be changed." After that "things are automatically going to happen."

NOVEMBER 1941

On November 28, the two Japanese envoys walk with Cordell Hull to the White House for talks with President Roosevelt.

DECEMBER 6

Foreign Minister Shigenori Togo informs Kurusu and Nomura that Japan is sending its final reply to the U.S. Government. They were instructed to present the 14-point memorandum the next day at exactly 1:00 p.m. (7:30 a.m. in Honolulu). But delays in typing up the final part, which was to sever all negotiations, moved the meeting to 2:00 p.m.

9

The envoys arrived at the State Department having no knowledge that the attack in Hawaii was already in progress. Hull learned of the attack on Pearl Harbor from the President moments before greeting the two diplomats. Hull politely read the memorandum knowing its words were meaningless. He coldly turned to Nomura and Kurusu telling them that the 14-part note was full of lies and distortions. Nomura tried to answer, but Hull silently waved the embarrassed men out of his office. Neither diplomats knew the two nations were at war until they returned to their Embassy.

Here is what an exasperated Secretary Hull stated to Japanese Ambassadors:

335

December 7, 1941

Secretary of State Hull and Ambassador Nomura

The United States never had knowledge that Pearl Harbor was to be attacked. All eyes were pointed towards Southeast Asia where a Japanese fleet was known to be on the move. The U.S. knew war was imminent, but did not know when, where or how. Japan's plan was to break off relations with the U.S. one half-hour before the surprise attack on Pearl Harbor. But due to a transcription problem at the Japanese Embassy, the formal ultimatum to end the embargo was delivered over an hour late by Nomura and Kurusu. Neither Ambassadors were aware that the attack on Pearl Harbor was already in progress.

"I must say that in all my conversations with you during the last nine months. I have never uttered one word of untruth. This is borne out absolutely by the record. In all my fifty years of public service I have never seen a document that was more crowded with infamous falsehoods and distortions, on a scale so huge that I never imagined until today that any Government on this planet was capable of uttering them."

Cordell Hull
Secretary of State

SECRET CODES:

Breaking complex Japanese Diplomatic codes was not an easy task for American Intelligence. A new Japanese code machine was dubbed "Purple" by U.S. code breakers and was introduced in the Summer of 1939. U.S. Army and Naval Intelligence units, including many of Japanese-American descent, worked tirelessly to decipher nearly impossible coded messages whose encrypted language was made up of approximately 33,000 symbols, numbers and words. Messages to and from Tokyo and its embassies never mentioned Pearl Harbor nor at any time indicated that Japan was planning to attack the United States.

PEARL HARBOR BOMBED
Diplomatic Negotiations Fail

10

U.S. LEADERS OF DEFENSE

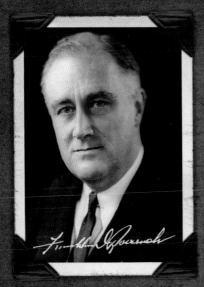

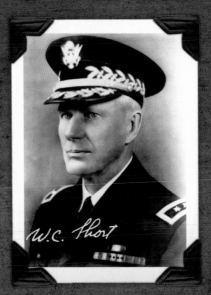

PRESIDENT FRANKLIN DELANO ROOSEVELT

President of the United States of America and Commander in Chief of all U.S. Military forces from March 1933 until his death in April 1945. He would lead the United States out of the economic crisis of the Depression and through the most difficult days of World War II.

REAR ADMIRAL HUSBAND E. KIMMEL

Commander in Chief of the U.S. Pacific Fleet beginning in February 1941. Kimmel believed that the most direct threat of an attack on Pearl Harbor came from the nearby Japanese bases in the Marshall Islands. Kimmel was held responsible for the unpreparedness of U.S. naval forces on December 7, and was relieved of command on December 17, 1941.

LIEUTENANT GENERAL WALTER C. SHORT

General Short commanded the Army's Hawaiian Department and oversaw the coastal defense of the Hawaiian Islands. The Army was responsible for defending the U.S. Pacific Fleet when in port. This included protecting the Pearl Harbor Navy Base and its oil tanks, dry docks and repair and storage facilities.

SECRETARY OF STATE CORDELL HULL

Appointed by President Roosevelt in 1933, Hull conducted the fateful diplomatic negotiations with Japan's Ambassadors Nomura and Kurusu in the fall of 1941. However, there was little chance that American and Japanese positions would be reconciled.

JAPANESE LEADERS OF WAR

PRIME MINISTER
HIDEKI TOJO

VICE ADMIRAL
CHUICHI NAGUMO

ADMIRAL
ISORUKU YAMAMOTO

EMPEROR
HIROHITO

General Hideki Tojo conceived and guided the Japanese war machine. He held numerous high-level positions including Prime Minister of Japan beginning in October 1941, Minister of War and Chief of Staff of the Army through 1944. Tojo ordered the attack on Pearl Harbor and was responsible for hundreds of thousands of deaths throughout Asia, China and the Pacific.

Flying his flag on the carrier Akagi, Nagumo was the Commander in Chief of the First Air Fleet and would successfully lead the Japanese Strike Force, or "Kido Butai," from northern Japan to attack Pearl Harbor. With their mission accomplished, Nagumo's forces returned home in triumph.

In January 1941, Yamamoto conceived the plan for the Pearl Harbor attack. As Commander in Chief of the Combined Japanese Fleet he believed that a decisive aerial raid against the U.S. Pacific Fleet would shift the strategic balance in Japan's favor and protect the flank of Japan's Southern Operation into Southeast Asia.

Japanese tradition considered Hirohito a direct descendant of the ancient sun goddess Amaterasu and his subjects revered him as a god. While he reluctantly gave his approval to attack Pearl Harbor in 1941, he cautioned the Japanese Supreme Court Command about the dangers of war with the United States and recommended negotiations first.

January 7

Recognizing continued opposition by the U.S. to Japan's presence in China, Admiral Isoruku Yamamoto, Commander in Chief of Japan's Navy, begins to draft plans to neutralize the United States Pacific Fleet which includes a surprise attack on Pearl Harbor.

January 27

Rumors begin to surface that Japan is planning a surprise attack on Pearl Harbor. Neither the American Ambassador to Japan, Joseph Grew, nor Washington gives credence to the report, since Grew's source was unreliable.

March 27

Takeo Yoshikawa, a spy for Japanese Naval Intelligence, arrives in Honolulu. For the next 8 ½ months he gathers information on U.S. ships and planes.

July 24

The Japanese occupy French Indochina despite continuing opposition from the United States.

DEAN JANUARY MARCH APRIL JULY

MADE IN ENGLAND

January 23

The newly appointed Japanese Ambassador, Kichisaburo Nomura, sails to America where he serves until the bombing of Pearl Harbor. Until the day of the bombing of Pearl Harbor, he was uninformed about the surprise attack.

"KATE" Torpedo Bomber

April 10

Admiral Osami Nagano is appointed chief of the Japanese Navy. General Staff and Vice Admiral Chuichi Nagumo is appointed Commander of the First Air Fleet. The First Air Fleet is organized into three carrier divisions comprising hundreds of aircraft.

July 26

In retaliation for Japanese aggression, President Franklin D. Roosevelt freezes all Japanese funds on deposit in America.

F.D.R.

Ambassador Nomura and Envoy Kurusu meet with news reporters at the White House.

JAPA

Prime Minister Tojo

第7図 Carrier Akagi

1938年(昭和13年)大改装後の赤城
Akagi, 1938.

October 17

General Hideki Tojo appointed the new Prime Minister of Japan by the Emperor and also retains his position as Minister of War.

November 2-3

In a pre-dawn dress rehearsal near Ariake Bay, Kyushu, Japanese war planes and ships simulate their planned attack on Pearl Harbor."

November 26

The carrier task force leaves Japan for Hawaii under the command of Vice Admiral Chuichi Nagumo. U.S. Secretary of State Cordell Hull meets with Diplomats Nomura and Kurusu to discuss the U.S. demand that Japan withdraw from China and Indochina.

December 2

The Japanese task force crosses the International Date Line without being detected and is now halfway to Hawaii. In the last of several Imperial Conferences, Emperor Hirohito gives his consent to an all-out war.

December 7

At 6:20 a.m. Commander Fuchida led the first wave comprised of 183 planes towards Pearl Harbor. By 1:00 p.m. all surviving Japanese aircraft were back aboard their carriers and returning to Japan.

OCTOBER   NOVEMBER   DECEMBER

October 18

Admiral Osami Nagano, chief of Japan's Naval General Staff, gives his approval for Admiral Yamamoto's plan for Pearl Harbor.

November 15

Japan sends diplomat Saburo Kurusu to Washington D.C. to assist Ambassador Nomura in negotiations with U.S. Secretary of State Cordell Hull. If peace negotiations are unsuccessful, Japan intends to wait until the end of the month before ordering the Oahu attack.

November 23

Admiral Nagumo holds a briefing aboard the Akagi for all unit commanders and flying officers to inform them of plans to attack the U.S. Fleet in Pearl Harbor.

November 29

Suspecting that Japan is close to war, Secretary Hull urges President Roosevelt, who is vacationing in Warm Springs, Georgia, to return to Washington.

December 6

Recognizing the apparent failure of diplomatic efforts between the United States and Japan, President Franklin D. Roosevelt prepares and sends a personal appeal to Emperor Hirohito which goes unanswered.

SUNDAY EVENING, DECEMBER 7, 19

TTACKS U.S

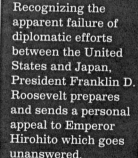

Cmdr. Minoru Genda, an advocate of carrier aviation, developed Admiral Yamamoto's plan to attack the U.S. Fleet at Pearl Harbor into a successful tactical operation.

14

FLASH BULLETIN

THE WORLD THIS DAY WITNESSED A NEW TYPE OF WEAPONRY THAT WOULD CHANGE HISTORY...

THE JAPANESE GOVERNMENT

On Sept. 6, 1941 Emperor Hirohito was pushing his cabinet, led by Premier Prince Konoye, to make every effort for a diplomatic solution first, rather than choose war. The Japanese Army and Navy continued preparing for war while at the same time putting up a pretense of diplomacy.

Japan committed a task force of 32 vessels for the attack on Pearl Harbor including the carriers *Akagi, Hiryu, Soryu, Kaga, Zuikaku* and *Shokaku*. Dubbed the "Kido Butai" (Strike Force), this naval armada was secretly assembled in late November at Hitokappu Bay in northern Japan under command of Vice Admiral Chuichi Nagumo.

Aichi "VALS" ready for take off from the SHOKAKU.

Anti-aircraft guns on the carrier ZUIKAKU. AKAGI visible in background.

Soryu being built at Kure, Japan. Was completed in December 1937.

Pilots go over mission details prior to launch.

.IT WAS THE BEGINNING OF LARGE SCALE AIRCRAFT CARRIER BASED WARFARE.

"Akagi" Red Dragon circa, 1940

Hideki Tojo

TELEGRAM
CLIMB MT. NIITAKA=DECODED

...CODED PRE-ARRANGED MESSAGE THE JAPANESE FLEET RECEIVED FROM TOKYO ON

DEC 2, 1941 TO ATTACK PEARL HARBOR WAS: CLIMB MT. NIITAKA... THE FLEET WAS

940 MILES NORTH OF MIDWAY ISLAND... MOUNT NIITAKA WAS THE HIGHEST PEAK IN

THE JAPANESE EMPIRE AND SYMBOLIZED JAPAN'S DETERMINATION TO CLIMB

THE MOST DANGEROUS MOUNTAIN OF ALL TIME...THIS MESSAGE SIGNALED THE FINAL

DECISION TO WAGE WAR AGAINST AMERICA.   [1941 DEC 2 AM 8:2..]

THE QUICKEST, SUREST AND SAFEST ...

ニイタカヤマノボレ
*Niitakayama Nobore - Climb Mt. Niitaka

Flight crews ready Kate bombers of the 2ⁿᵈ wave for takeoff from the carrier Akagi, Admiral Nagumo's flagship.

16

Commander
Mitsuo Fuchida

The Japanese Fleet set sail for the Hawaiian Islands at 6 a.m. on November 28, 1941. To avoid detection a northern approach was selected. It would be the least traveled shipping route in the winter months due to rough and stormy seas.

機動部隊
Kido Butai
(Strike Force)

IMPERIAL JAPANESE NAVY

伊号潜水艦と特殊潜航艇
358 Feet
I-CLASS SUBMARINE WITH MIDGET SUB

駆逐艦　漣
388 Feet
DESTROYER SAZANAMI

軽巡洋艦　香取
425 Feet
LIGHT CRUISER KATORI

給油船　健洋丸
520 Feet
OILER KENYO MARU

重巡洋艦　筑摩
661 Feet
HEAVY CRUISER CHIKUMA

高速戦艦　霧島
730 Feet
BATTLESHIP KIRISHIMA

航空母艦　赤城
855 Feet
AIRCRAFT CARRIER AKAGI

0   100   200   300   400   500   600   700   800   900

No. 9

JAPANESE TASK FORCE:

6 - Aircraft Carriers with 432 Aircraft
2 - Battleships
2 - Heavy Cruisers
2 - Light Cruiser
11 - Destroyers
9 - Oilers

SPECIAL ADVANCE FORCE:

30 - I-Class Submarines
5 - Midget Submarines

JAPANESE ATTACK POSITION:

230 miles North of Oahu

TARGET:

U.S. Pacific Fleet at Pearl Harbor

"KATE" torpedo bomber taking off from SHOKAKU

The crew readies a "ZERO" fighter for launch

DECEMBER 7, 1941

It was a quiet, sunny Sunday morning with American forces going about their normal weekend routines. Kido Butai, the Japanese strike force of six aircraft carriers with 432 aircraft aboard, two battleships, two heavy cruisers, two light cruisers, nine destroyers and three I-Class submarines had taken up its position 230 miles north of Oahu.

The first wave of attack aircraft -- 183 planes in all, rolled off the decks of the Japanese aircraft carriers at 6:00 a.m. This first wave sped towards Pearl Harbor led by Commander Fuchida. Immediately, the carrier crews readied for the second wave. 167 aircraft began launching from their carriers. It was a little after 7:00 a.m. The Nakajima B5N2 "KATES" were followed by the Aichi D3A1 "VAL" dive bombers and the Mitsubishi A6M2 Reisen "ZERO" fighters.

*Aircraft carrier SORYU-- stern

Second wave of Japanese planes prior to takeoff

2nd wave -- 167 aircraft -- 7:05am... a "ZERO" fighter

departs aircraft carrier SORYU

Commander Mitsuo Fuchida (center) was chosen to train the Japanese pilots and organize the air strike against Pearl Harbor. Flying as an observer in a Nakajima "KATE" bomber (piloted by Lt. Mutsuzaki), Cmdr. Fuchida led the first wave of 183 planes to attack the U.S. Pacific Fleet.

眞珠灣攻擊の機動部隊航跡圖
TRACK OF CARRIER TASK FORCE FOR PEARL HARBOR ATTACK
(一九四一年十一月二十六日より十二月二十三日迄)
26 NOVEMBER-23 DECEMBER 1941

TWO WARNINGS MISSED

On Oahu, two warnings of the impending attack were missed. The first occurred in the waters just outside the entrance to Pearl Harbor at 6:45 a.m. The destroyer *Ward* fired on, depth-charged and sank an unidentified submarine within the defensive sea area. The second warning occurred at 7:02 a.m. when two Army radar operators at the Opana station above Kahuku Point on Oahu's North Shore picked up a large formation of planes on their radar screens. After checking their equipment, they notified the watch officer at Fort Shafter. No action was taken because the officer believed the planes to be a flight of American B-17's flying in from California.

TORA! TORA! TORA!

ISLAND OF OAHU

FIRST WAVE 0740 HOURS

SECOND WAVE 0840 HOURS

1

KAHUKU POINT Radar Station

2

3

4

WHEELER Army Airfield

PEARL HARBOR Ford Island

5

KANEOHE Naval Air Station

7

6

HICKAM Army Airfield

10

BELLOWS Army Airfield

EWA MARINE CORPS Air Station

8

9

11

HOSPITAL

The first wave of planes attacked Wheeler Field at 7:50 a.m. Japanese fighters and bombers quickly spread to the other military airfields on the island -- Ford Island, Hickam, Ewa, Kaneohe, Bellows as well as Pearl Harbor.

Within two hours, American air power in Hawaii was immobilized. At Pearl Harbor, the Japanese planes struck and neutralized the U.S. Pacific Fleet in 15 minutes. Battleships California, Oklahoma, West Virginia, Nevada and Arizona were sunk, as was the old battleship Utah, then being used as a target and anti-aircraft training vessel. The battleships Maryland, Tennessee and Pennsylvania were damaged. Initially, the American response to the attack was sporadic, but within five minutes American vessels began to fire back.

"AIR RAID, PEARL HARBOR. THIS IS NOT DRILL!" WAS RELAYED TO THE U.S. FLEET.

Water geysers mark torpedo hits on battleships OKLAHOMA and WEST VIRGINIA at Battleship Row.

6 ♣

Japanese Torpedo Bomber
Mitsubishi Type 97
"Kate"

9 ♣

"Zero"

Japanese Fighter
Mitsubishi Type 0
"Zeke"

A ♣

It was nearly 10:00 a.m. when the first wave of Japanese aircraft began landing on their carriers. By noon, the last planes had returned. Admiral Nagumo felt that their mission was successful even though the fuel tank farms, dry docks and repair facilities were never bombed. His carriers were running low on fuel and not knowing where the American aircraft carriers were, he reversed course for Japan. The decision to forgo a third wave assault and not attack the fuel storage tanks and ship repair facilities, proved to be a major blunder in Japan's plan to neutralize America's Pacific Fleet. Doing so would have added several more years to Pearl Harbor's recovery.

Dec. 7

As the second wave withdrew, the main objective of the attack — immobilizing the Pacific Fleet — had been accomplished. American casualties included 2,388 killed and 1,178 wounded. Twenty-one vessels of the Pacific Fleet had been sunk or damaged, and 75 percent of the planes on the airfields surrounding Pearl Harbor were damaged or destroyed.

Continued on Page B, Column 8

U. S. NAVAL COMMUNICATION SERVICE
U. S. S. WASP
Norfolk Navy Yard—12-17-40—50,000
7 DEC 41   JR

NS3   2 DF2 1832 0F3 0F4 1F0 0

U R G E N T

AIRRAID ON PEARLHARBOR X THIS IS NOT DRILL

**INCOMING RADIO

Radio Message sent to all U.S. naval ships around the world

TOR: 1936/TW/17.8
TOR: 1536 SHIPS TIME

CAPT NOTIFIED
EXEC NOTIFIED

From: Action To: Info. To: STATION FILE
COM PACIFIC FLT   COMATLANTIC FLT   Release

20

"JAKE" SEAPLANE

AICHI E13A1 NAVY TYPE-0

At 5:30 a.m. on December 7, 1941, the cruisers Chikuma and Tone each catapulted into darkness an Aichi E13A1 "JAKE" float plane to scout the anchorages at Pearl Harbor and Lahaina Roads, Maui. The planes would then scout for about 15 minutes to insure that their reports were accurate. Their message back to the fleet on the morning of December 7, broke the spell of radio silence that had prevailed since November 26, 1941 when the Japanese fleet had sortied.

"JAKE" Sea Plane early 1941

"JAKE" FLOAT PLANE

MISSION: RECONNAISSANCE

- Single engine, twin-float reconnaissance seaplane
- Crew consisted of a Pilot, Navigator/Radioman and a Rear Gunner
- Armament - 7.7mm machine gun
- Speed 138 mph / Range 1,300 miles or 15 hours

'21

Lahaina Anchorage

TELEGRAM

"CLOUD CEILING OVER ENEMY FLEET"

THE CHIKUMA'S FLOAT PLANE REPORTED THE PRESENCE OF THE U.S. FLEET IN

PEARL HARBOR AND RADIOED BACK THE TOTAL NUMBER OF VESSELS IN PORT

AND THEIR CLASSIFICATION..."CLOUD CEILING OVER ENEMY FLEET, 1700 METERS"

WAS PART OF THE SPECIFIC COMMUNICATION...

THE QUICKEST, SUREST AND SAFEST WAY TO SEND MONEY IS BY TELEGRAPH OR CABLE

PACIFIC FLEET LUCKY
...TO BE BASED AT PEARL HARBOR

When Admiral Kimmel took over command of the Pacific Fleet in February 1941, one of his first duties was to abandon the fleet anchorage at Lahaina Roads, Maui for fear of submarine attacks. Had the Pacific Fleet been anchored at Lahaina, it would have been the primary target of the Japanese Strike Force, as Japan's planes would have had greater aerial maneuverability to attack. Scouting Lahaina on December 7, two "JAKES" and the submarine I-72 confirmed that there were no vessels at the anchorage and that they were in fact at Pearl Harbor. Had the U.S. Pacific Fleet been moored in Lahaina's deep waters, far greater devastation would have prevailed! Rescue efforts or any potential salvage of ships would have been impossible. Therefore, an attack on Lahaina Anchorage would have proven to be a total loss for the Pacific Fleet!

Ironically, the Pacific Fleet being based at Pearl Harbor was a stroke of luck!

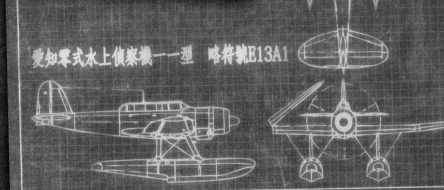

愛知零式水上偵察機一一型　略符號E13A1

A B5N2 "Kate" flying a training sortie, Japan 1939.

Japan Declares War on U.S.

DIVE BOMBER "VAL"

Val Dive Bomber
Spreads Its Wings In The Pacific

The Japanese Navy, in the summer of 1936, issued a specification call for a carrier-based airplane with dive-bombing capabilities. The leading manufacturers submitted designs. Mitsubishi, Nakajima, and Aichi received contracts to build prototypes. After several prototypes and the addition of enlarged wings, tail and stabilizers and a Mitsubishi air-cooled engine, the Aichi design was accepted by the Japanese Navy due to its great maneuverability.

9 ♣

Japanese Dive Bomber
Aichi Type 99 DB
"Val"

6 ♣

Aichi D3A1 Type 99 "VAL"

E II-2 06

報国-525
(第五八金日本號)

Aichi D31A "VAL"
Aircraft Carrier **Zuikaku**

DESCRIPTION:
Single engine, carrier-borne and land based bomber. All metal construction with fabric covered control surfaces on tail and wings.

CREW:
2 men: Pilot and Radioman/Rear Gunner in tandem enclosed cockpit.

ARMAMENT:
One 250kg (551lb) bomb under fuselage that was released via swing arm. Capable of carrying two 60kg (132lb) bombs under each wing. Two forward firing 7.7mm type 97 machine guns and a third in the rear cockpit.

ENGINE & SPEED:
Mitsubishi 1049 hp radial engine; 240mph with a range of 915 miles.

MISSION:
The "VAL" was designed to dive bomb targets including ships, structures or parked aircraft.

MANUFACTURER:
Aichi Kokuki K.K., Nagoya

Of the 129 **"VALS"** used in the
Pearl Harbor attack, 15 were shot down.

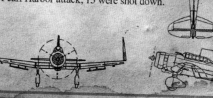

IN THE PRE-DAWN LIGHT...

The first bombs to fall on Pearl Harbor came from Lt. Commander Kakiuchi Takahashi's attack group of dive bombers that struck the PBY ramp at Ford Island.

Why were the Japanese Aircraft given "Nicknames"?

The numbering system used by Japan to catalog its various aircraft was difficult for Americans to remember and often there were conflicting interpretations. In 1942, U.S. Army Intelligence assigned each type of Japanese aircraft a simple English name to make identification and reporting easier. Thus, the Aichi E13A1 Type 0 Seaplane was dubbed "JAKE", the Aichi D3A1 Type 99 Dive Bomber was named "VAL" and the Nakajima B5N2 Type 97 was nicknamed "KATE". All fighter planes were given masculine names and other aircraft such as bombers and patrol planes were given feminine names.

350 aircraft roared off the decks of their rolling and pitching aircraft carriers in 2 separate waves.

Destination: Pearl Harbor. Here a burning "VAL" pulls up in desperation over the oiler, Neosho tied up along Battleship Row.

"KATE" TORPEDO/HIGH LEVEL BOMBER
NAKAJIMA B5N2

33-66 Feet

Torpedo Speeds to Target at Preset Depth	Japanese Pilots Had To Do 3 Things	Average Harbor Depth 40 Feet
	• Keep Plane's Nose Horizontal to Sea • Attack Speed 160 Knots • Drop Torpedoes 33-66 Feet Above Water	

A TORPEDO FROM AN AIRPLANE...?

A critical element of the Japanese plan was the successful development of a torpedo that could be used in the shallow waters of Pearl Harbor. Instead of a torpedo being fired from a submarine, it would be dropped by a low flying plane, speed through the water and explode against the ship's hull below the waterline. The pressure of seawater combined with the explosive charge maximized destruction of the targeted ship.

Japanese Torpedo Bomber
Nakajima Type 97 MK.3 TB
"Kate"

9 ♣

Torpedoes used in the attack had to be modified by adding wooden fins for Pearl Harbor's 40-foot shallow waters.

In 1932, the Japanese began develop a series of carrier atta bombers capable of deliver torpedoes as well as bombs. Th aircraft was a single eng monoplane with a sleek low-wi design that surpassed Japane expectations. The "KATE" exceed air speed of 230 miles per hou At this point in history Jap possessed the finest high lev torpedo bomber in the world.

Half the Japanese attacking for was made up of "KATES", a total 143 planes. 40 torpedo bombe were used in the first wave bombing. The remaining 1 aircraft were high-level bomber In just 15 minutes, the ma battle line of the U.S. Pacif Fleet was smashed. The "KATES" we responsible for most of the dama to Pearl Harbor and its ships.

中島 九七式艦上攻撃機 B5N

TORPEDO AWAY!!!

40 TORPEDOES WERE CARRIED INTO PEARL HARBOR ALTHOUGH ONLY 36 WERE ACTUALLY DROPPED.

25 HIT THEIR TARGETS

4 MISSED THEIR TARGETS

6 DROPPED INCORRECTLY

2 PLANES WERE SHOT DOWN BEFORE DROPPING

1 MALFUNCTIONED

1 REPORTED AS LOST

1 STILL UNACCOUNTED FOR

Nakajima "Kate" over Pearl Ha

"ZERO" CARRIER-BASED FIGHTER PLANE

MITSUBISHI A6M2 TYPE-0

A New Fighter Design

The Japanese Imperial Navy was looking to design a fighter aircraft that could:

- Carry two 132 lb bombs
- Capable of sustained speeds of 331 mph
- Climb and maneuver quickly
- Cruise for 6 to 9 hours
- Armed with two 20mm cannons and two 7.7mm machine guns
- Take off in less than 230 feet
- Out perform any fighter that Japan had flown before!

HOW DID THE "ZERO" GET ITS NAME?

Gaining its infamous nickname from its serial number: A6M2, Navy Type "0" Model 21. In 1940-41 the "ZERO" was the most feared fighter plane of the time. The "ZERO's" role at Pearl Harbor was to protect the bombers and torpedo planes from attack by enemy pursuit planes and to control the skies over Pearl Harbor.

IT IS ESTIMATED...

that the Japanese Navy had 521 fighter planes, 328 were "ZEROs". A force of 79 "ZEROs" were sent to bomb Pearl Harbor and nine were lost in action. This force effectively neutralized American air power on Oahu in less than two hours.

Mitsubishi "Zero" fighter was considered by aviation experts to be the finest aircraft of type in 1941. With its surprise attack on ber 7, 1941, this aircraft ushered the U.S. war. Over 10,000 "Zero" fighter planes were between 1939 and 1945.

D HOWARD HUGHES DESIGN THE "ZERO"?

he mid-1930's, Howard Hughes designed an raft called the "H-1". He offered it to the Army claiming it to be the fastest plane in sky. To prove this, he flew it from California New Jersey at an average speed of 332 mph. s record stood for nearly 10 years. But, the ny turned down his offer and Japan's subishi Ltd. bought his plans and used many the "H-1" innovations in designing their d World War II plane, the "ZERO."

三菱 零式艦上戦闘機 A6M2

Although the Pearl Harbor attack was conceived as an air strike, the plan was modified to test the newly developed "Type A" midget submarines. These five "midgets" would be carried piggy-back across the Pacific Ocean on the decks of 5 modified Japanese I-Class submarines. They were designated the "Special Attack Unit."

JAPANESE "MIDGET" SUB
HA-19

0 1 2 3 4 5 6 7 8 9 10
SCALE - FEET

Figure 1

Each submarine was 80 feet long, 6 feet wide and powered by electric storage batteries that were not rechargeable. Each midget sub was to be carried on the deck of a "mother" submarine and deployed when within range of its designated target. The crew consisted of one junior officer who was the pilot, plus one crewman. It carried two 18-inch torpedoes. Its range for travel was approximately 100 miles.

OAHU

MIDGET SUB RECOVERY SITES

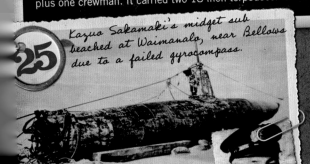

(25) *Kazuo Sakamaki's midget sub beached at Waimanalo, near Bellows due to a failed gyrocompass.*

Kazuo Sakamaki
First U.S. Prisoner of War

Midget Sub Timeline
December 7, 1941...

THE MISSION:

The mission of the "Special Attack Unit" was for the five midget submarines to covertly slip into Pearl Harbor under the cloak of darkness and lie in wait until the aerial attack was over and then launch their torpedoes. Reaching their destination on December 5, 1941, the mother subs closed within 10 miles off Pearl Harbor and launched the first midget sub at midnight December 6. The last to launch was at 3:33 a.m. and headed for the lights of the harbor entrance. When their mission was completed they would sail submerged counterclockwise around Ford Island, escape out to sea and rendezvous with their mother subs 7 miles off Lanai Island.

American sailors examine a Japanese midget submarine raised in 1960 from Keehi Lagoon. It was returned to Jap

3:42 a.m.
he first midget submarine as sighted. The minesweeper SS *CONDOR* spotted a eriscope located 1.75 miles outh of the Pearl Harbor entrance. The destroyer USS *WARD* was notified and arched without success.

6:30 a.m.
The USS *ANTARES* spotted a submarine following them. The sub's conning tower was exposed. A PBY patrol plane dropped smoke pots near the sub a few minutes later.

6:40 a.m.
The *WARD* spotted the midget submarine behind the *ANTARES*. The sub was making a run for the harbor at approximately 12 knots.

6:45 a.m.
The No.1 gun of the *WARD* opened fire and missed. Immediately the No. 3 gun fired, hitting the submarine at the conning tower's junction with the hull. The submarine heeled to the starboard, slowed and sank. The *WARD* depth-charged the sinking vessel as it plunged 1,200 feet down.

8:17 a.m.
The destroyer USS *HELM* spot another midget sub hung up on coral reef on the western side of the channel entrance. The *HEL* fired upon the submarine but it submerged and slipped away.

SECRET SUB

特殊潜航艇の攻撃

*attacks by special underwater vessels

While the submariners were venerated as the "heroes of Pearl Harbor" by Japanese and German propagandists, their actual record was dismal. The midget subs did not achieve much success at Pearl Harbor. At night, on December 7 and 8, the mother I-Class submarines met at the rendezvous point, but the midgets did not return. Japanese attack planners originally feared that the presence of the midget submarines would give away their intentions, but the U.S. forces did not understand the significance of the midget submarine sightings within the Pearl Harbor defensive zone until it was too late.

The 9 honored submariners

Naoji Iwasa LEADER

Masaharu Yokoyama   Shigemi Furuno

Shigenori Yokoyama   Akira Hiroo

Naokichi Sasaki   Tei Ueda

Yoshio Katayama   Kiyoshi Inagaki

The 10th pilot, Ensign Sakamaki, was disgraced in Japan, becoming a U.S. prisoner and was not included in painting.

TELEGRAM

WHO FIRED THE FIRST SHOT, SANK THE FIRST SHIP AND TOOK THE FIRST PRISONER OF WAR?

IN THE EARLY HOURS OF DECEMBER 7TH, 1941, U.S. FORCES SPOTTED, FIRED UPON AND SANK A JAPANESE 2-MAN MIDGET SUBMARINE. LATER IN THE MORNING, JAPANESE ATTACK FORCE BOMBED PEARL HARBOR DEVASTATING THE U.S. FLEET. BUT OFFICIALLY THE UNITED STATES FIRED THE FIRST SHOTS, SANK THE FIRST SHIP AND CAPTURED THE FIRST PRISONER OF WAR AGAINST JAPAN

THE QUICKEST, SUREST AND SAFEST WAY TO SEND MONEY IS BY TELEGRAPH OR CABLE

RESTRICTED

Shipyard workers at Mare Island Navy Yard examine Ensign Sakamaki's midget sub in September 1942 that was captured and brought to the mainland. The sub toured 41 states helping to sell war bonds.

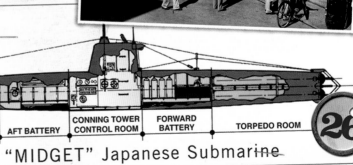

8:30 a.m.

Inside the harbor, the USS ZANE, a minesweeper, spotted a midget near Berth X-23. CinCUS sent out the alert at 8:32 a.m., "Japanese submarine in Harbor."

8:36 a.m.

The seaplane tender USS CURTISS opened fire on a midget sub inside the harbor. The midget sub sunk after she was rammed and depth-charged by the destroyer USS MONAGHAN.

| MOTOR ROOM | AFT BATTERY | CONNING TOWER CONTROL ROOM | FORWARD BATTERY | TORPEDO ROOM |

TYPE A "MIDGET" Japanese Submarine

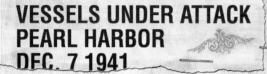
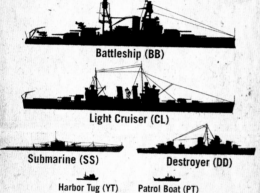
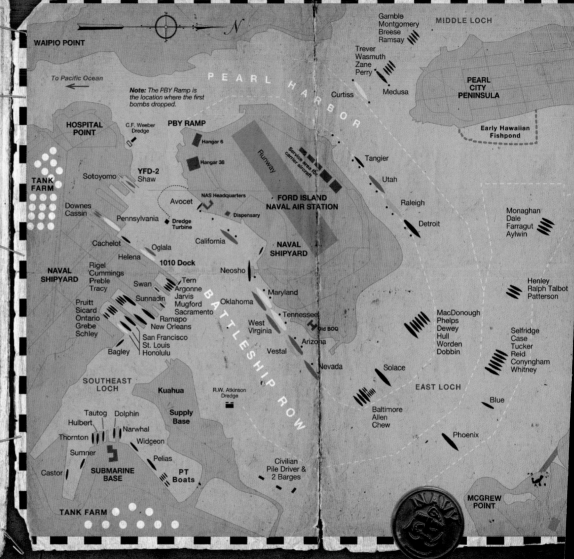

PEARL HARBOR: *December 7, 1941 7:55 a.m.*

U.S. BATTLESHIPS SMASHED

21 SHIPS SUNK OR DAMAGED

HONOLULU, Dec. 8. Japanese bombers bearing the insignia of the Rising Sun appeared over Honolulu about 7:55 a.m. (Honolulu time) yesterday morning and wrecked havoc on American Army and Navy bases. "...Among the scorched and twisted hulls, the worst casualty is the battleship ARIZONA having taken a deadly blow and is now burning beyond recognition... thousands aboard have perished."

Also sunk and severely damaged are the battleships NEVADA, WEST VIRGINIA and OKLAHOMA, as well as the CALIFORNIA docked on the south end of Battleship Row. The PENNSYLVANIA, proud flagship of the fleet was badly hit while in dry dock. MARYLAND and TENNESSEE also linger in critical condition from the attack.

PEARL HARBOR UNDER ATACK

Japanese "KATE" torpedo bomber in action with "VAL" dive bomber striking the U.S. Fleet early Sunday morning December 7th.

BOMBS TAKE TOLL ON HAWAII

In the worst surprise attack in the history of the United States, Japanese planes furiously descended upon Pearl Harbor yesterday, smashing the prime defense line of American might.... our beloved battleships.

America's armed forces were the only thing standing in the way of Japan's insatiable desire for power and natural resources. Japan was prepared to do anything to hold off America. Yesterday, they did the unthinkable. With stealth and a premeditated attack plan, Japan took thousands of American lives.

CASUALTY NUMBERS WERE KEPT AT A MINIMUM EARLY ON SO AS NOT TO CAUSE UNDO ALARM TO THE AMERICAN PEOPLE, PLUS NOT TO HAVE THAT INFORMATION KNOWN TO THE JAPANESE.

WAR EXTRA
DEVASTATION AT PEARL
Naval Base at Pearl Harbor Hawaii, Attacked

TOKYO DECLARES WAR ON U.S.

WASHINGTON, Dec. 8. — The White House announced today that the Japanese attacked Hawaii with heavy damage and probable heavy loss of life is to be

AMERICAN PACIFIC FLEET STRIKES BACK AT JAPAN

HONOLULU, Dec. 8. — Japanese Fleet of Aircraft Carriers and dozens of support vessels sneak

USS WEST VIRGINIA torpedoed

Battleship settles on harbor bottom

The sinking USS WEST VIRGINIA alongside the USS TENNESSEE framed by clouds of oily smoke.

Disregarding danger of explosions, a yardcraft pumps water into the burning USS WEST VIRGINIA.

Okie lies submerged next to USS MARYLAND at Battleship Row.

USS *Oklahoma-capsized*

The OKLAHOMA rolled over when it was struck by nine torpedos.

Wreckage of the destroyers USS DOWNES (L) and USS CASSIN (R) in Dry Dock One with the damaged USS PENNSYLVANIA.

Damaged seaplanes

...ning ships from Ford Island

PEARL HARBOR
122
EMPLOYEE

PEARL HARBOR
7083
EMPLOYEE

Sunken hull of the minelayer USS OGLALA

Dry Dock One

30

This is 9:30 in the morning!

Japanese bombs hit the destroyer USS SHAW in the floating dry dock. Flames reached the forward ammunition magazine erupting in a spectacular explosion.

Explosion on the USS HELENA ruptured OGLALA'S hull causing it to capsize from extensive flooding. Heavy black smoke at right is from the burning USS SHAW.

Ford Island, Hangar 6

Hangar 6 consumed by fire after bombing

USS SHAW'S bridge was a total loss from fire and explosions.

U.S. MARINE CORPS AIR STATION
STATION
PATROL
EWA, OAHU, T.H.

31

Black smoke darkens the skies over the Marine Barracks.

HEAVY DAMAGE

Fort Kam

Wreckage of Japanese Zero that crashed at Fort Kamehameha.

Marine sits in shock.

P-40 at Wheeler Field

W-KO (12-7-41)

Burned out wreckage of a
P-40 Army fighter plane.

172

Beacon of hope, the proud flag of the USS CASSIN
survived unharmed in Dry Dock One.

Civilians Killed, Wounded

Called back to work,
four civilian shipyard
riggers were killed.

onel from an errant anti-aircraft shell exploded close

Sailors at Kaneohe Naval Air Station
fight fires on a burning PBY patrol plane

AFTER ALL FIRES WERE OUT...

USS WEST VIRGINIA lies sunk in the mud of the harbor bottom.

A flight of twelve B-17 bombers from California...

...arrived during the attack and were assaulted by Japanese fighters.

NAVY YARD 72 PEARL HARBOR

NAVY YARD 51 PEARL HARBOR

NAVY YARD 81 PEARL HARBOR

Wreckage of a "VAL" recovered from harbor.

Heavy casualties suffered

Charred remains of field tents and Hangar One at Wheeler Field.

W-HD (12-7-41) AB

124875

33

over 400 men were trapped inside...

B-17 bomber crash landed at Bellows Field

Standing on the capsized hull of the USS OKLAHOMA, workers frantically cut into the ship to rescue trapped sailors. Only 32 were rescued.

HAWAIIAN AIR DEPOT
4500

B-17 bomber was forced down at Bellows Field by attacking enemy "ZEROs".

After the attack, ordinary citizens, like Frank J. Barnett Jr. moonlighted at the Hawaiian Air Depot and guarded Hickam and Wheeler Fields. Known as the Civilian Defense Unit, they wore khaki uniforms and even carried rifles.

Following the attack, damaged aircraft were bulldozed for the massive clean-up operation.

Shattered remains of Hangar 11

34

Hickam Field hangar was destroyed by Japanese bombing.

Wheeler Field wreckage of destroyed Army fighter planes.

AMERICAN LOSSES

Casualties:	2,390 killed	1,178 wounded
Planes Lost:	169 destroyed	159 damaged

Killed
Navy – 1,999
Marines – 109
Army – 233
Civilians – 49
Total = 2,390

	SUNK	DAMAGED
Battleships	Arizona	Maryland
	California	Pennsylvania
	Nevada (beached)	Tennessee
	Oklahoma	
	West Virginia	
Destroyers	Cassin	Helm
	Downes	
	Shaw	
Cruisers:		Helena
		Honolulu
		Raleigh
Training Ships:	Utah	
Mine Layer:	Oglala	
Seaplane Tender:		Curtiss
Repair Ship:	Vestal (beached)	
Floating Dry Dock:	YPD-2	
Tug:	Sotoyomo	

Over 185 vessels were anchored within the Pearl Harbor basin on the day of the attack. Twenty-one were either sunk or damaged. Of these 21 vessels, all but 3, the USS OKLAHOMA, USS ARIZONA and the USS UTAH, were returned to active service before the end of the war.

CONTINUED from Page C, Column 2 - The Destroyers, USS CASSIN, DOWNES and SHAW were not "officially" sunk because the dry dock was empty of water. They were considered destroyed. After water was pumped into the dry dock they were listed as "sunk."

JAPANESE LOSSES

Casualties:	55 Airmen killed in action
Planes Lost:	29 total
	(9 fighters, 15 dive bombers, 5 torpedo bombers)
Midget Subs:	4 lost, 1 captured

Midget Sub Crewmen: 9 crewmen lost, 1 taken prisoner of war and disgraced by the Japanese Navy for having dishonored his country by surrendering rather then choosing death.

Type I-Class Sub was sunk by planes from the USS ENTERPRISE 200 miles northeast of Oahu on December 10, 1941. I-70's complement was 80 officers and men. While the loss was considered by the Japanese as a casualty from the "Hawaii Operation", it was not a loss directly from the December 7th attack.

JAPANESE STRIKE FORCE

The Japanese strike force consisted of six carriers, two battleships, two heavy cruisers, one light cruiser, nine destroyers, five I-class submarines, five midget submarines and eight oil tankers. Vice Admiral Nagumo (Commander in Chief of the First Air Fleet) launched 350 aircraft of the 432 carried by the six aircraft carriers. Only 29 (8% of the total force) were shot down.

rain MOORE-McCORMAC

At Kaneohe Naval Air Station, after the sounds of battle have faded away, it is time to bury the dead and heal the wounded. A marine squad renders honors to their fallen comrades.

36

POSTCARD
This Space may be used for Correspondence.

POSTAGE.

Lt. Kermit Tyler, Officer on Duty at Fort Shafter Information Center had been told, that if the Honolulu radio station KGMB was playing music on the radio during the night, a fleet of B-17's could be expected. At 3:00 a.m. on his drive to work, Tyler tuned into KGMB and in fact heard music being aired.

American air fleets utilized the radio station airwaves as a directional beam that served as a homing guidance system for travel towards Oahu.

FOR ADDRESS ONLY.
Mariann Shevitz
Box 354 Route #7
Baltimore, Maryland

It was Lt. Tyler's second day on the job!

Pvt. Joseph L. Lockard with the radar receiver that plotted the incoming planes.

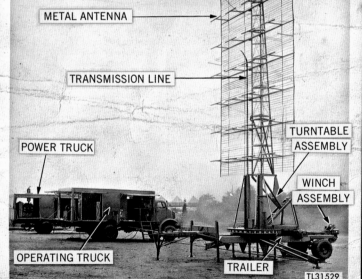

METAL ANTENNA

TRANSMISSION LINE

POWER TRUCK

OPERATING TRUCK

TURNTABLE ASSEMBLY

WINCH ASSEMBLY

TRAILER

TL31529

Early in the morning on December Privates George Elliot and Joseph Lock were still on duty at the Opana Mob Radar Station located in the north mountains near Kahuku Point. At 7:02 t noticed a very large blip on the ra screen and promptly called the Ra Information Center at Fort Shafter to rep the unidentified planes. Lt. Kermit Ty the only officer on duty believed it was incoming flight of B-17 Flying Fortr bombers from California. He calmly t them, "Well, don't worry about it."

At the time the Army privates reported sighting, the Japanese planes w approximately 132 miles from their Pe Harbor target!

37

All radar stations operated only in the early morning hours by order of General Short. The truck to pick up Elliot and Lockard the morning of December 7th was late. Voluntarily, they decided to continue practicing with their equipment. Radar Information Center personnel on duty promptly closed down at 0700.

RADAR?

ADAR:
HE ELECTRONIC SENTRY

SCR-270-B Mobile Radar Units were mounted on van-type trucks and were set up on Koko Head, Kaaawa, Kawailoa, Opana and Fort Shafter. The lack of experience with this new technology and erratic readings led to false alarms. When the report came in from Fort Shafter, Lt. Kermit Tyler believed it was an expected flight of incoming B-17's. He felt justified in not taking further action. Tyler made an educated guess about the radar blips based upon the following:

The USS ENTERPRISE was returning to Hawaii and was approximately 215 miles west of Oahu. A group of its carrier aircraft were flying into Pearl Harbor that morning.

Army planes from Hickam Field were flying practice maneuvers.

An expected Fleet of B-17's were flying into Hickam from the West Coast that morning.

Three PBY Catalina seaplanes were out on a routine anti-submarine patrol that morning. These planes were expected to return to Kaneohe Navel Air Station.

EXPERIMENTAL
TECHNOLOGY

At the time of the bombing at Pearl Harbor radar technology was experimental, not nearly as proficient as it is today. Not many people even knew how it worked, much less how to operate it. The Opana mobile radar units were located 230 feet above sea level near Kahuku Point on the North tip of Oahu and operated every morning from 4 a.m. to 7 a.m. daily. General Short firmly believed these were the most dangerous hours for an aerial attack. Some navy ships also had radar but it could not be used when in port due to heavy interference from the mountains that surrounded Pearl Harbor.

Island of Oahu Radar Stations

Opana
Kawailoa
Kaaawa
OAHU
Pearl Harbor
Fort Shafter
Koko Head

CLARA

DINAH

34   35

38

ISLAND OF
OAHU

ORIGINAL TRACKING PLOT OF APPROACHING AIRCRAFT INTO OAHU ON DECEMBER 7TH AT 7:20AM. IT WAS A VERY LARGE UNIDENTIFIED FLIGHT AND WAS THE LARGEST "BLIP" THEY HAD EVER SEEN.

PRIDE OF THE PACIFIC FLEET

One of the most fortunate strokes of luck for the United States on December 7, 1941 was the absence of all three aircraft carriers assigned to the Pacific Fleet at Pearl Harbor.

U.S. AIRCRAFT CARRIERS

Admiral Yamamoto was concerned from the outset about the American naval air fleet and its potential threat to his attacking forces. That is why the American carriers were made the priority target. On average, a carrier could hold up to 90 planes. Yamamoto was greatly disappointed when the scout planes observed no carriers in port on that fateful morning. Japanese pilots then focused on the battleships that were moored along Battleship Row.

USS SARATOGA (foreground) and USS LEXINGTON (behind) with Diamond Head Crater in the background. Pilots were having a hard time telling the two LEXINGTON Class carriers apart. So, the Navy placed a vertical stripe on the "SARA's" smoke stack, distinguishing it from her sister ship, USS LEXINGTON.

USS Saratoga seen at sea level with crew on deck

USS ENTERPRISE
CV-6 "Wildcats"

TELEGRAM

U.S. CARRIERS: LOCATION UNKNOWN

..THE DECISION TO END THE ATTACK AND NOT TO LAUNCH A THIRD STRIKE ON

PEARL HARBOR WAS HEAVILY INFLUENCED BY THE THREAT OF

THE AMERICAN CARRIERS' UNKOWN LOCATION...

1941 DEC AM 9:47   *a stroke of luck!*

39

THE QUICKEST, SUREST AND SAFEST WAY TO SEND MONEY IS BY TELEGRAPH OR CABLE

The USS ENTERPRISE was scheduled to arrive at Pearl Harbor on the morning of December 7th. Fortunately, turbulent seas and stiff winds forced Admiral Halsey's task force to reduce speed. The ENTERPRISE was approximately 215 miles west of Oahu when the attack unfolded and did not enter Pearl Harbor until the morning after the attack.

SBD DAUNTLESS DIVE BOMBER
This aircraft carrier-borne dive bomber and scout plane was unsurpassed as one of the U.S. Navy's most superior dive bombing aircrafts.

OUT TO SEA

[A]dmiral Husband Kimmel felt [th]at any threat to the Hawaiian [Is]lands would come from the [w]est. In an effort to strengthen [th]ose defenses, he ordered Admi[ra]l William Halsey's "Task Force [8]" to Wake Island to drop off a [M]arine Fighter Squadron. Task [F]orce 8 included the carrier USS [E]nterprise and a cluster of cruis[er]s and destroyers. It departed on [No]vember 28, 1941.

[O]ne week later, on December 5, [19]41, the USS Lexington and her [es]corts, known as "Task Force 12", [un]der the command of Admiral [Jo]hn H. Newton, departed for [Mi]dway to deliver fighter planes.

[O]n the West Coast of the United [St]ates the carrier USS Saratoga [co]mpleted a routine refit at Puget [So]und Naval Yard. The carrier [sa]iled from San Diego on Decem[be]r 8, 1941, for Pearl Harbor to [li]n[k] up with the Lexington and [En]terprise.

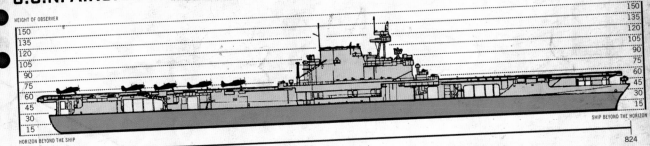

U.S.N. AIRCRAFT CARRIER

HEIGHT OF OBSERVER

HORIZON BEYOND THE SHIP

SHIP BEYOND THE HORIZON

USS ENTERPRISE CV-6
IDENTIFICATION AND CHARACTERISTICS - OCTOBER, 1938

SPECIFICATIONS (As built. 1938)

DISPLACEMENT:	19,800 tons (STANDARD)
DIMENSIONS:	824' x 108'
WATERLINE TO DECK:	53 feet
WATERLINE TO MAST:	143 feet
POWER PLANT:	4 Parson's single reduction geared steam turbines powered by 9 Babcock & Wilcox 400 psi boilers
HORSEPOWER:	120,000 HP T
SPEED:	32.5+ knots
FUEL CAPACITY:	6,500 tons (more than 1.5 million gallons)
ENDURANCE:	10,400 nautical miles at 15 knots
ARMAMENT:	8 X single 5 inch-38 caliber dual purpose guns; 4 X quad 1.1 inch-75 caliber cannons; 24 X .50 caliber machine guns
AIRCRAFT:	96 maximum

AIRWING (Squadrons & Aircraft)

VS-6 (Scouting Squadron 6)
SBD Dauntless

VB-6 (Bombing Squadron 6)
SBD Dauntless

VT-6 (Torpedo Squadron 6)
TBM Devastator

VF-6 (Fighting Squadron 6)
F4F Wildcat

UPDATES

40

THE JAPANESE SUCCESS AT PEARL HARBOR FORCED THE U.S. NAVY TO REEVALUATE THE VERY WEAPON THE JAPANESE STRIKE FORCE [U]SED TO DESTROY THE PACIFIC FLEET...THE AIRCRAFT CARRIER.

"JUST ANOTHER EASY DAY"

On the eve of December 6, Lieutenants Kenneth M. Taylor and George S. Welch, dressed in tuxedos, had attended a formal dance at the Officer's Club at Hickam Field. They left around 11 p.m. and drove back to the Bachelor's Officer Quarters at Wheeler Field. The usual Saturday night poker game at the BOQ was in full swing so they sat in to play. Welch turned in early. Close to 4 a.m. a weary Taylor left the game to hit the sack thinking Sunday would just be another easy day.

Lieutenants Taylor and Welch, America's first air hero's of WWII

The men in the BOQ were suddenly awakened the morning of December 7, by the sounds of roaring planes and loud explosions. Someone yelled "We're under attack!" Taylor, still in his tuxedo pants and a skivvy shirt, ran to the window and saw clouds of smoke and fire rising from the twisted wreckage on the flight line where the squadron's fighter planes were parked wingtip to wingtip for anti-sabotage protection. continued..

Kittyhawk

PBY Catalina

68 "Cats" were based on Oahu on December 7. With the exception of 12, all were destroyed or damaged during attack

U.S. PLANES AT

Grumman F4F-3-U.S. Navy Fighter

CONSOLIDATED PB2Y-2 NAVY PATROL BOMBER.

KEEP 'EM FLYING!

Pearl Harbor

B-17 FLYING FORTRESS CROSSING PACIFIC ENROUTE TO P.H.

It was the approaching Japanese bombers on their way to Pearl Harbor that the only officer on duty at Fort Shafter's information center mistook as the Hawaii bound flight of B-17's arriving from California. Unarmed and low on fuel the B-17's arrived during the attack and forced to land where they could. One had to land on a golf course.

Huge Douglas Bomber
U.S. Army B-18A

22 destroyed,
11 got airborne

27 27

Douglas SBD Dauntless
DIVE BOMBER

GIVE 'EM HELL!

42

December 7, 1941

U.S.S. ARIZONA DESTROYED

Aunt Susan's neighbor Bobby A. was on board Dec. 7

Missing — Prayers...

IN THE NEWS

HONOLULU, Dec. 9. — There will never be another ship in the United States Navy that will bear her name, for out of respect, the *Arizona's* title has been retired. The dreadful loss of life and the retention of so many souls within her hull has made the ship an icon of American history. Today the sunken ship has been honored by a white marble memorial, built directly above her, known as the *Arizona* Memorial.

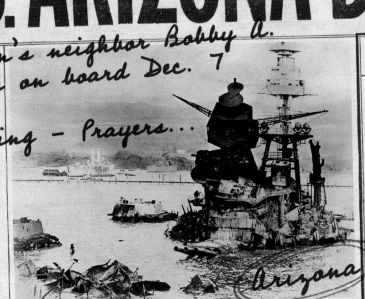

Arizona

Of all the ships attacked on December 7, 1941, the *Arizona* received the most damage. The explosion of the forward magazine demolished the front two-thirds of the ship. The USS *Arizona* was so badly damaged that it could not be repaired even though salvaging ships was a priority at that time.

USS ARIZONA BB-39

CLASS: Pennsylvania Class Battleship

LENGTH: 608 feet

WEIGHT: 34,400 tons

ARMAMENT: Twelve 14-inch guns mounted in 4 turrets

CREW: 1,512 officers and men

CASUALTIES: 1,177 sailors and marines; Approximately 900 still entombed.

MOORED DURING ATTACK: Battleship Row at Berth Fox-7.

*The repair ship **USS Vestal** was moored outboard.

A GALLANT SHIP

HONOLULU, Dec. 9. — Many of the *Arizona's* crew had liberty on Saturday, December 6, 1941. However, the majority of the men returned to the ship by midnight. More than 50 lucky crew members remained on shore. At the time of the attack, the *Arizona* was moored at berth F-7, with the repair ship *Vestal* alongside.

About 8:06 a.m. the USS *Arizona* took its death blow. A single 1,760 lb. bomb hurtled through the air reportedly striking near turret No. 2 and penetrating deep into the battleship's interior before exploding near the forward magazine. With a tremendous blast the *Arizona* blew up. Most of the men aboard were killed. The blast blew men off the decks of neighboring ships and threw tons of debris into the air and into the harbor. 1,177 sailors and marines were killed on that fateful day. 230 bodies were ultimately recovered; 900 are still entombed.

War Bulletins

BERLIN, Tuesday, Dec. 9 — AD NB dispatch from Tokyo today said Japanese imperial navy headquarters announced an American airplane mother ship had been sunk off Honolulu. (The Japanese had previously claimed an American aircraft carrier sunk in Sunday's attack.)

MELBOURNE, Australia, Tuesday, Dec. 9 — ...lia declared war on Japan today.

LONDON, Dec. 8 — The emigre government of Greece, following Britain's lead, declared war on Japan tonight. The Greek am... in Tokyo was instructed to ask for his passports.

BERLIN, Dec. 8 — A DNB dispatch from Tokyo tonight said the "espionage department" had arrested 100 persons of "unrevealed nationality" in Japan.

GUATEMALA CITY, Dec. 8 — Guatemala allied herself...

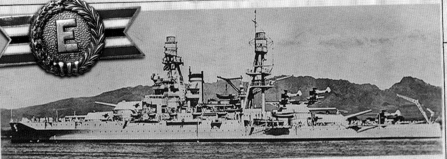

Above: Profile of a gallant ship—the Mighty USS *Arizona* sails through Pearl Harbor before the attack.

On June 19, 1915, Miss Esther Ross from Arizona christened the newest battleship, taking two beribboned bottles in each hand, one of pure Arizona water, the other traditional champagne and hurled both bottles against the bow shouting, "I name thee ARIZONA!" It was estimated well over 50,000 people attended the launching at New York Navy Yard.

Over 1 million pounds of gunpowder stored on the ship ignited into a fiery explosion that blew through 3 decks.

BROTHERS IN ARMS...

There were 36 sets of brothers and one father/son on board. 24 sets of brothers died during the explosion, as did the father/son. During this time, the Navy implemented new guidelines to separate brothers from serving together on the same ship.

The USS ARIZONA (BB-39) steams down the East River, leaving New York City in 1916. This was her 1st "shakedown cruise", testing the ship's performance as well as acquainting the crew with its capabilities.

U.S.S. ARIZONA REMEMBERED

Throughout the war the **USS ARIZONA** served as an unofficial memorial and was rendered honors by passing ships, a practice that ships continue to this day. Since March 7, 1950 the raising and lowering of colors over the Arizona has been carried out daily by Navy and Marine personnel.

THE UNITED STATES OF AMERICA
MEDAL OF HONOR

THREE CREW MEMBERS OF THE USS ARIZONA WERE CITED FOR "CONSPICUOUS GALLANTRY ABOVE AND BEYOND THE CALL OF DUTY" FOR THEIR ACTIONS ON DECEMBER 7 1941.

CAPTAIN FRANKLIN VAN VALKENBURGH
USS ARIZONA'S COMMANDING OFFICER (POSTHUMOUSLY)

REAR ADMIRAL ISAAC C. KIDD
COMMANDER BATTLESHIP DIVISION ONE (POSTHUMOUSLY)

LT. COMMANDER SAMUEL G. FUQUA
USS ARIZONA'S SENIOR SURVIVING OFFICER

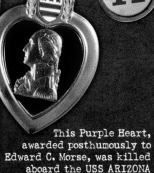

This Purple Heart, awarded posthumously to Edward C. Morse, was killed aboard the USS ARIZONA on December 7, 1941.

USS California (BB-44) *"The Prune Barge"*

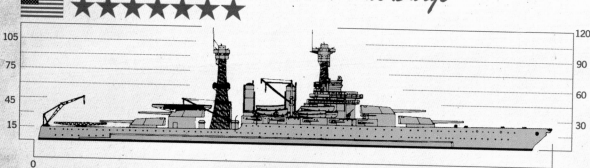

★★★★★★★

TENNESSEE CLASS BATTLESHIP (1920)

LENGTH — 624 feet
WEIGHT — 32,300 tons
MAIN ARMAMENT — twelve 14-inch guns mount
    in 4 turrets.
CREW — 1,546 officers and men
CASUALTIES — 102 officers and crewmen
MOORED DURING ATTACK — Battleship Row, Qu
    F-3 by herself.
REFLOATED AFTER ATTACK — March 24, 1942
RETURNED TO ACTIVE DUTY — May 5, 1944, lef
    west coast for the invasion of Saipan

History

The USS CALIFORNIA was the flagship of the Pacific Fleet and the Battle Fleet from 1921 to 1941. Affectionately nicknamed the "Prune Barge" as a tribute to its home state's crop of plums, which become prunes when dried. On December 7th, she was struck by two torpedoes and one 551 lb. bomb resulting in a serious fire that killed 6 officers and 92 sailors. Flooding of the vessel was slow but progressive. Two factors played into the loss of the CALIFORNIA:

1. Prior to the attack, many manholes and vents were opened for inspection. This compromised the vessel's watertight integrity. Due to these large openings plus ruptured pipelines, water and oil permeated the vessel causing the crew to abandon the fire and engine rooms.

2. An oil fire from the USS ARIZONA spread down to the CALIFORNIA, resulting in a temporary abandonment of the ship at its most critical moment when the crew was attempting to keep the CALIFORNIA afloat. Eventually, the crew returned and counter flooded the ship to correct a list of 16 degrees. The vessel was able to avoid capsizing due to these actions and she settled upright on the bottom three days later.

Back to War

Only one incident did mar the successful salvage of the CALIFORNIA. Two weeks before the ship went into drydock, a powerful explosion ripped the CALIFORNIA. Gasoline vapor had built up in a fuel storage compartment and was ignited by a bare light bulb with defective wiring. The result was the loss of a window frame patch. Seven months later, the USS CALIFORNIA steamed back to the West Coast and underwent further repair work and modernization at Puget Sound Naval Yard, Washington. On May 5, 1944, the USS CALIFORNIA was completely modernized and she sailed for Saipan, ready for active duty with the Fleet.

Completely re-built and modernized and ready for action USS *California* heads out to sea painted in dazzle camouflage.

Final Salute

Her flag was hauled down for the last time on February 14, 1947. She was sold in March, 1959 to The Boston Metal Co., Baltimore, Maryland for $860,000 and broken up for scrap.

NOTES: *California received seven battle stars for her service in World War 2.*

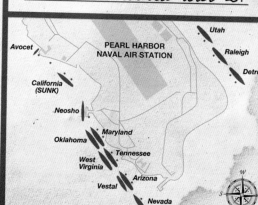

PEARL HARBOR
NAVAL AIR STATION

Utah
Avocet
Raleigh
Detro
California (SUNK)
Neosho
Maryland
Oklahoma
Tennessee
West Virginia
Arizona
Vestal
Nevada

45

A AIR MAIL

CALIFORNIA is listing to port from torpedo and bomb damage.

CALIFORNIA was flagship of Commander, Battle Force, Vice Admiral William S. Pye.

SS CALIFORNIA ALVAGED

timately, the USS *California* as evaluated for salvage and pair. The first task was to ghten the ship's load. All n-essential material including el, ammunition, machinery, econdary gun batteries and guns om most of the turrets were emoved. Salvage workers placed offerdams around the ship's orecastle and quarterdeck. Water as then pumped out of the looded spaces and the *California* as refloated on March 24, 1942.

MEDAL OF HONOR

ISSUED UNDER THE PROVISIONS OF THE ACT OF CONGRESS

Three crew members of the USS CALIFORNIA were cited for
"conspicuous gallantry above and beyond the call of duty"
for their actions on December 7.

- **Chief Radioman Thomas J. Reeves** (Posthumous Award)
- **Machinist's Mate Robert R. Scott** (Posthumous Award)
- **Gunner Jackson C. Pharris**

All three received the Nation's highest award, the Congressional Medal of Honor.

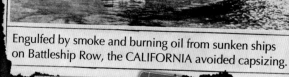

Engulfed by smoke and burning oil from sunken ships on Battleship Row, the CALIFORNIA avoided capsizing.

USS Maryland (BB-46) *"Lucky Mary"*

131
120
90
60
45
30
15
0   624

* PROFILE AFTER REPAIRS

MARYLAND CLASS BATTLESHIP (1917)

LENGTH — 624 feet
WEIGHT — 32,693 tons
MAIN ARMAMENT — Eight 16-inch guns mounted
in 4 turrets.
CREW — 1,496 officers and crewmen
CASUALTIES — 2 officers and 2 enlisted men
MOORED DURING ATTACK — Battleship Row at
berth F-5, inboard of the USS Oklahoma
LEFT PEARL HARBOR — December 20, 1941
(ship not sunk)
RETURNED TO ACTIVE DUTY — February 26, 1942

History

The USS MARYLAND sustained minor damage from one bomb that struck the port side of its hull below the water line and one bomb that struck the deck, killing 2 officers and 2 enlisted men. This flooded several compartments but never threatened the ship. A caisson was placed around the damage to the hull and by December 20, 1941 she sailed to the Puget Sound Navy Yard for final repairs.

Compared to the damage sustained by the other battleships, MARYLAND's damage was minimal due to her position inboard of the USS OKLAHOMA.

Back to War

The MARYLAND returned to the fleet for active duty on February 26, 1942. After a second overhaul in 1944, she was fully modernized and set sail for the Pacific arena.

Ready to rejoin the fleet after repairs USS *Maryland* departs Puget Sound Navy Yard. The *Maryland* would earn seven battle stars in World War Two.

NOTES:

-2-

Casualties from U.S.S. Maryland
Killed in action 12/7/41

- BRIER, Claire R. (USN)   - CROW, Howard D. (USN)
- GINN, James B. (USN)   - McCUTCHEON, Warren H. (USN)

Aboard vessel during Pearl Harbor attack.
Declared dead by War Dept.   12/41

Final Salute

On July 8, 1959, the USS MARYLAND was sold for scrap to the Learner Corporation of Oakland, California for $676,777 and broken apart at the Todd Shipyards. During the war, the "Lucky Mary" steamed a total of 152,697 miles and spent a total of 76 days in actual combat between the years of 1942-1945.

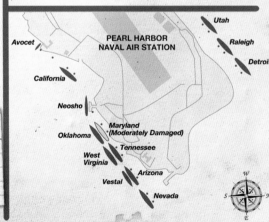

PEARL HARBOR NAVAL AIR STATION

Avocet
Utah
Raleigh
Detroit
California
Neosho
Maryland (Moderately Damaged)
Oklahoma
Tennessee
West Virginia
Arizona
Vestal
Nevada

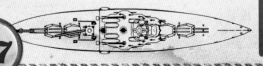

PHOTO ABOVE: The lightly damaged MARYLAND and the capsized hull of the OKLAHOMA. Crew from the MARYLAND would assist in the rescue of 32 men from the overturned ship when holes were cut into the hull. Note: The smoke is from the burning USS WEST VIRGINIA and USS ARIZONA. The MARYLAND did not have serious fires.

U.S.S. MARYLAND

AUTHORIZED August 29, 1916
KEEL LAID April 24, 1917
LAUNCHED March 20, 1920
COMMISSIONED July 21, 1921

Built by
Newport News Shipbuilding & Dry Dock Co.
Newport News, Va.

FOURTEENTH ANNIVERSARY OF COMMISSIONING

1921 - JULY 21 - 1935

U.S.S. MARYLAND

1935
JUL 21
10.00 A.M.

BIRTHDAY!

CALIFORNIA PACIFIC INTERNATIONAL EXPOSITION
1935-SAN DIEGO-1935

PHOTO ABOVE: Departing from the Brooklyn Navy Yard in the 1930's for a training cruise. Naval Academy cadets take in the sights as the MARYLAND sails down New York City's East River.

USS Nevada (BB-36) *"The Cheer-Up Ship"*

★★★★★★★

NEVADA CLASS BATTLESHIP (1911)

LENGTH — 583 feet

WEIGHT — 30,500 tons

MAIN ARMAMENT — Ten 14-inch guns mounted in 4 turrets

CREW — 1,390 officers and men

CASUALTIES — 57 men killed, 109 wounded

MOORED DURING ATTACK — Moored singly at Battleship Row, Berth F-8;

RETURNED TO ACTIVE DUTY — Ready for action by December, 1942.

121
90
75
60
45
30
15
0   583

* PROFILE AFTER REPAIRS

History

On December 7, 1941, at 7:55 a.m., the ship's 24-man band was gathered on USS NEVADA's quarterdeck for the raising of Morning Colors. As they began playing "The Star Spangled Banner" the first bombs reverberated around the Pearl Harbor Naval Station. Not a man broke formation, even under fire, until the final note of the National Anthem died away. At 8:03 a.m. the ship was struck by a torpedo.

Known as The "Cheer-up" Ship, this legend explains the Nevada's nickname: as she got underway during the height of the Japanese onslaught and moved down the channel, she sailed past devastation and destruction of Battleship Row. In proud excitement, the men on nearby ships cheered at the sight of NEVADA's heroic effort to reach the open sea.

In World War Two the "Cheer-up Ship" saw action in both the Pacific and European theaters of war. Those operations earned *Nevada* seven battle stars.

Back to War

On February 12, 1942, the NEVADA was refloated and sent to Dry Dock Two. There, the ship received temporary repairs and was made seaworthy for the voyage to Puget Sound Navy Yard, Washington. It arrived on May 1, 1942 and was reconditioned and modernized. In late December, 1942, it rejoined the Pacific Fleet.

NOTES:

Final Salute

The NEVADA survived Pearl Harbor, the Aleutian Campaign, the North American Patrol, the Normandy Landings, the Invasion of Southern France, Okinawa and even an atom bomb explosion when she was chosen as the target for Operation Crossroads at Bikini Atoll in July of 1946. She was decommissioned August 29, 1946 and ultimately sunk as a target off Hawaii on July 31, 1948 by rockets, torpedoes and gunfire from U.S. ships.

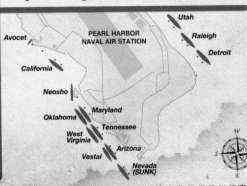

Utah
Raleigh
Detroit
PEARL HARBOR NAVAL AIR STATION
Avocet
California
Neosho
Maryland
Oklahoma
Tennessee
West Virginia
Vestal
Arizona
Nevada (SUNK)

THE VESSEL WAS STRUCK BY ONE TORPEDO AND FIVE 55l LB. BOMBS

WO FROM USS NEVADA ECEIVE MEDAL OF HONOR

o men from the USS NEVADA were arded the Medal of Honor for traordinary courage and disregard r their own personal safety: hief Boatswain **Edwin J. Hill** and achinist **Donald K. Ross**.

ONTINUED ON 2A

The USS NEVADA was the end vessel at Battleship Row and the only battleship to get underway during the attack. She quickly became a target for Japanese dive bombers. Many of her crew would be cited for heroism in their attempt to get their ship to the open sea. NEVADA's gallant dash ended at Hospital Point by orders to intentionally beach the ship to prevent it from sinking in the harbor channel due to a torpedo hit. Later that morning, yard tugs moved the NEVADA across to Waipio Peninsula.

LEFT: Fighting fires on the NEVADA aground off Hospital Point
MIDDLE: Damage to ship's forward main deck from bomb explosions
RIGHT: Huge hole on NEVADA's port bow from torpedo hit

Donald K. Ross

Edwin J. Hill

PHOTO LEFT: Battered and barely afloat NEVADA is nudged into Dry Dock Two for repairs to make the ship seaworthy for the voyage to the West Coast.

50

USS *Oklahoma* (BB-37) *"Okie"*

115
105
90
75
60
45
30
15
0
583

NEVADA CLASS BATTLESHIP (1911)

LENGTH — 583 feet
WEIGHT — 30,500 tons
MAIN ARMAMENT — Ten 14-inch guns mounted in
4 turrets
CREW — 1,270 officers and men
CASUALTIES — 429 men killed
MOORED DURING ATTACK — Battleship Row, Berth
F-5, Outboard of the USS Maryland.

NEVER RETURNED TO ACTIVE DUTY

History

As the Japanese torpedo planes made their initial runs on Battleship Row, the USS OKLAHOMA received much of their attention. It was estimated that 9 torpedoes struck the vessel during the first 10 minutes of the attack. Damage was so extensive that the OKLAHOMA capsized at its berth less than 15 minutes after the first torpedo hit.

Many men were still trapped in the OKLAHOMA after it capsized. Tapping sounds and voices could be heard from within the ship's overturned hull. A rescue party made up mostly of civilian Navy Yard personnel, working tirelessly for nearly 40 hours, cut through sections of the ship's bottom and saved the lives of 32 men. The last man was rescued at 2:30 A.M. on December 9th. Julio De Castro, Joe Bulgo and 18 others from Shop 11 would receive Navy Citations for their heroic efforts "with utter disregard of their own personal safety."

Rescue & Recovery

The sheer size of the OKLAHOMA and the ship's poor condition made salvage questionable. It was important to rid the harbor of this immobilized ship and make the berth at F-5 available for other ships. By May 1942, contractual agreements were made between the Navy and Pacific Bridge Company to complete the job. Turning over the OKLAHOMA, it was said, was the most technically difficult task faced by the salvage division at Pearl Harbor. The righting operation began on March 8, 1943 and took three months to complete. During this period, the grim task of removing nearly 400 bodies was concluded.

In the years before the war, USS *Oklahoma* was a familiar sight operating in Southern California and Hawaiian waters.

Final Salute

In November 1943, the ship was re-floated and moved into Dry Dock Two for repairs. Work also continued in removing its remaining auxiliary machinery, stores, 14-inch guns and ammunition. With new classes of battleships appearing in the fleet, it was not worth the effort and expense to restore the badly damaged OKLAHOMA to active service. In 1946, she was sold for scrap for $46,000. In May 1947, the "Okie" left Pearl Harbor for the last time under tow by two tugs. The OKLAHOMA's final end came several days later when she began taking on water. The tow lines were released and she sank to the quiet depths of the Pacific Ocean, 540 miles northeast of Oahu.

Neosho
Oklahoma (SUNK)
Maryland
Tennessee
West Virginia
Arizona
Vestal
Nevada

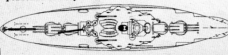

...ahoma Seconds Before Disaster!

BB-37

Some historians believe it was the Japanese midget sub I-16tou that inflicted grave damage with its 2 torpedo hits to the USS OKLAHOMA causing the ship to capsize at its berth.

December 7, 1941

52

USS OKLAHOMA PROBABLY TOOK 9 TO 11 TORPEDOS

U.S.S. OKLAHOMA BB-37

Two members of the ship's crew were awarded the Congressional Medal of Honor posthumously for their actions on December 7, 1941:

Ensign Francis C. Flaherty
Seaman First Class James R. Ward.

James R Ward

Francis Charles Flaherty

BATTLESHIP PENNSYLVANIA STEAMS OVER 146,000 MILES

FIRE MAIN RISER

FR 85

When destroyer DOWNES exploded a half-ton section of torpedo mount landed on the forecastle of PENNSYLVANIA

The USS Pennsylvania is located in the background in Dry Dock One. Destroyers USS Downes (left) and USS Cassin (right) lay decimated in the foreground, like so many other vessels after the attack.

REPORT OF JAPANESE RAID ON PEARL HARBOR, 7 DECEMBER 19

"A 500-lb bomb dropped from an high-altitud bomber and penetrated the boat deck. Aft passing through this deck, the bomb eith deflected or rolled slightly in the compar ment before detonating... This detonati caused the boat deck to open up for a space about 20' X 20' opening... The bomb explosi in casemate No. 9, caused the death of abo 26 men and two officers."

- CINPAC Action Report Serial 0479 of 15 February 1942

The bow of the PENNSYLVANIA was badly scorched by burning fuel escaping from the ravaged destroyers.

1¢ POSTAGE
LONG MAY IT WAVE
UNITED STATES OF AMERICA

USS Pennsylvania (BB-38) *"The Mighty Penn"*

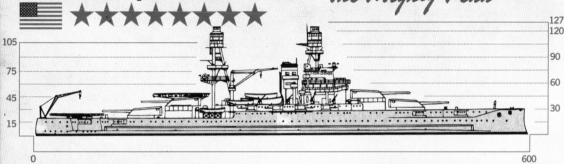

PENNSYLVANIA CLASS BATTLESHIP (1912)

LENGTH — 608 feet
WEIGHT — 34,400 tons
MAIN ARMAMENT — Twelve 14-inch guns mounted in 4 turrets
CREW — 1,395 officers and men
CASUALTIES — 24 men killed, 38 wounded
MOORED DURING ATTACK — Dry Dock One
RETURNED TO ACTIVE DUTY — March 30, 1942 after repairs and modernization

History

The PENNSYLVANIA was in Dry Dock One on December 7th to align its shafts and propellers. During the attack the battleship received minor damage. A 250 kg (551 lb.) bomb damaged a 5-inch 25-caliber anti-aircraft gun and then exploded one deck below. Another 5-inch gun was knocked out temporarily. The ship suffered fragmentation damage that compromised its splinter protection, deck, electrical gear, water mains and structural steel.

Back to War

In 13 days the damage was repaired and the 5-inch gun was replaced by one from the USS WEST VIRGINIA. On December 20, 1941 the ship sailed for San Francisco to complete repairs. The PENNSYLVANIA was ready for fleet service on March 30, 1942.

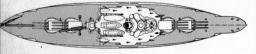

In 1941, "Pennsy" was the flagship of Admiral Husband E. Kimmel, Commander in Chief of the Pacific Fleet.

NOTES:

The Mighty Penn was awarded 8 battle stars for World War 2 service!

Final Salute

On August 12, 1945, just days before the surrender of Japan, the PENNSYLVANIA was torpedoed at Buckner Bay, Okinawa. She was the last major U.S. warship knocked out of action.

After the war, the "Mighty Penn" was used as an atomic bomb target for Operation Crossroads at Bikini Atoll in July of 1946. She was decommissioned August 29, 1946. The "Pennsy" was scuttled in deep waters on February 10, 1948.

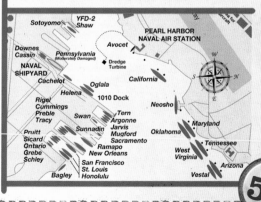

USS *Tennessee* (BB-43) *"Rebel"*

★★★★★★★★★★

*PROFILE AFTER REPAIRS

CALIFORNIA CLASS BATTLESHIP (1915)

LENGTH — 624 feet
WIDTH — 96 feet on December 7th - 114 feet after re-building
WEIGHT — 32,300 tons
MAIN ARMAMENT — Twelve 14-inch guns mounted in 4 turrets
CREW — 1372 officers and men
CASUALTIES — 5 men killed, 37 wounded
MOORED DURING ATTACK — Battleship Row, Quay F-6, inboard of USS West Virginia
RETURNED TO ACTIVE DUTY — February 25, 1942

History

During the attack, the USS TENNESSEE was struck by two large bombs. Both 1,760 pound projectiles broke up before proper detonation. One struck the center gun of turret No. 2 and the other pierced the roof of turret No. 3, rendering both turrets inoperable. The ship could not move from its mooring. When the outboard WEST VIRGINIA sank from its mortal wounds it pinned TENNESSEE hard against the mooring quay. The TENNESSEE was freed from its wedged-in position when the concrete mooring quays were dynamited by civilian contractors on December 16, 1941. The ship was moved to the Navy Yard in Pearl Harbor for minor repairs and ultimately onto the West Coast on December 20th for more permanent repairs. The ship was ready for sea duty on February 25, 1942.

Back to War

The TENNESSEE entered the Puget Sound Naval Yard on August 27, 1942, for a major modernization. The entire ship's superstructure above the main deck, with the exception of her 14-foot guns, was removed and completely rebuilt. Anti-torpedo defense blisters were added to the ship's hull increasing her beam to 114-feet, too wide to now pass through the 110-foot wide Panama Canal. On May 8, 1943, TENNESSEE emerged from the Navy yard a brand new battleship ready for her next mission with the fleet.

Odds & Ends

After TENNESSEE was repaired from the damage received at Pearl Harbor, the "Rebel" ship would next see action in Alaska during the Aleutians Campaign. TENNESSEE would participate in other major battles throughout the Pacific Theater of Operations earning the ship a Presidential Unit Commendation and ten battle stars for her outstanding service in wartime.

The "Rebel" steamed over 170,000 miles from December 7, 1941 to September 2, 1945.

Final Salute

The "Rebel" was ultimately placed in Reserve (Mothball Fleet) at the war's end and decommissioned in Philadelphia on February 14, 1947. Twelve years later on July 10, 1959, technology having passed her by, the USS TENNESSEE was sold for $724,999 to Bethlehem Steel Corporation of Baltimore, Maryland for scrapping.

whaleboat moves to rescue men om the oily waters.

TENNESSEE was wedged hard against the quays when the outboard WEST VIRGINIA sank. She was finally freed on December 16th.

HE FOUR YEARS OF WAR, THE USS TENNESSEE
D 9,347 14-INCH ROUNDS AND 46,341 SHELLS
NEMY POSITIONS FROM HER 5-INCH GUNS.

DIVISION OF NAVAL INTELL
Identification and Characteristic
JUNE, 1943

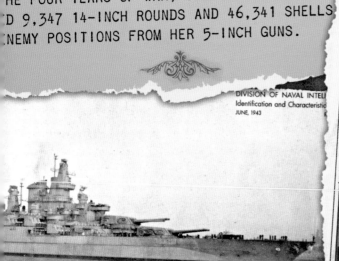

USS TENNESSEE'S COMMISSIONING, 631 TENNESSEANS ABOARD

While the ship was under construction, the state of Tennessee promoted a huge enlistment campaign throughout the state, using newspapers and posters on county courthouses in search of USS TENNESSEE's first crew. The enlistment was largely made up of volunteers throughout the state of Tennessee. On June 3, 1920, USS TENNESSEE's commissioning date, 631 Tennesseans came on board.

AFTER NINE MONTHS RE-BUILDING AT THE PUGET SOUND

NAVY YARD, TENNESSEE EMERGED TOTALLY

MODERNIZED AND READY FOR BATTLE.

Admiral Chester W. Nimitz, Commander in Chief U.S. Pacific Fleet, addressing the officers and men of USS *Tennessee* at Pearl Harbor on 17 November 1944 stated: "Your record that I have just reviewed is testimony to the great part you officers and men have made to the war in the Pacific. I salute each one of you on a fine record, a record everyone in the Navy can take pride in. Well done, *Tennessee*."

With war looming in Europe, the fleet is put on full alert. USS West Virginia is ordered to sea from New York City.

Mess Attendant Decorated For Pearl Harbor Heroism

May 27, 1942, Doris Miller, mess attendant first class aboard the USS WEST VIRGINIA, distinguished himself during the Japanese attack on Pearl Harbor, today was awarded the Navy Cross by President Roosevelt.

He was cited "for his distinguished devotion to duty, extraordinary courage and disregard for his own personal safety during the attack." On April 1, 1942, Secretary Knox's commendation described Miller's brave action as follows:

"While at the side of his captain on the bridge, Miller, despite enemy strafing and bombing and in the face of serious fire, assisted in moving his captain, who had been mortally wounded, to a place of greater safety, and later manned and operated a machine-gun until ordered to leave the bridge."

Miller, a resident of Waco, Tex., enlisted as a mess attendant third class at Dallas on September 16, 1939.

U.S.S. WEST VIRGINIA
VIEW LOOKING AFT AT AN ANGLE

CONFIDENTIAL
OFFICIAL PHOTOGRAPH

TELEGRAM

"GHOST SHIPS"

...OCT 25, 1944.. A JAPANESE FORCE OF 2 BATTLESHIPS, 1 CRUISER AND

4 DESTROYERS ENTERED SURIGAO STRAIGHT, PHILLIPINES AND WERE COMPLETELY

DESTROYED BY 5 AMERICAN "GHOST SHIPS" OF THE PEARL HARBOR ATTACK:

THE WEST VIRGINIA, MARYLAND, TENNESSEE, CALIFORNIA AND PENNSYLVANIA.

THE WEST VIRGINIA WAS FLYING THE SAME FLAG SHE HAD FLOWN

1944 OCT AM 7:50   ON DECEMBER 7, 1941.

THE QUICKEST, SUREST AND SAFEST WAY TO SEND MONEY IS BY TELEGRAPH OR CABLE

Obituary

Captain Mervyn S. Bennion Killed In Action

Though mortally wounded early in the attack, USS WEST VIRGINIA's Command Officer, Captain Mervyn S. Bennion was still involved in the defense of his sh He refused to leave the ship as he clung tenaciously to life. Captain Bennion w posthumously awarded the Medal of Honor for his conspicuous devotion to d extraordinary courage and complete disregard of his own life.

57 UNITED STATES LINE OF DEFEN

U. S. S.
NOV
18
A.M.
1941
WEST VIRGINIA

THE USS WEST VIRGINIA was the only ship from the Pearl Harbor atta

USS West Virginia (BB-48) *"The Wee Vee"*

★★★★★

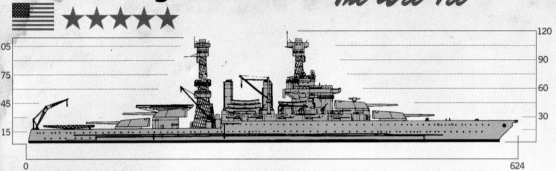

LENGTH — 624 feet
WEIGHT — 31,800 tons
WIDTH — 97 feet on December 7 — 114 feet after
modernization.
MAIN ARMAMENT — Eight 16-inch guns mounted in
4 turrets, 13.5 inch armor belt
CREW — 1,454 officers and men
CASUALTIES — 106 men killed
MOORED DURING ATTACK — Battleship Row, Quay
F-6, outboard of USS Tennessee
RETURNED TO ACTIVE DUTY — February 25, 1942

History

During the attack, the USS WEST VIRGINIA was moored just forward of the USS ARIZONA and berthed next to the USS TENNESSEE. As the outboard ship, the WEST VIRGINIA was hit by as many as 9 torpedoes and 2 bombs, killing 106 men. Quick thinking by Lt. Claude V. Ricketts, the Assistant Fire Control Officer, saved the ship from capsizing by counter-flooding so that the ship settled on an even keel in the mud of the harbor bottom. Counter flooding also saved the CALIFORNIA from capsizing but the OKLAHOMA rolled over too quickly to be saved by this method.

Damage to the "Wee Vee's" port side was so extensive that it raised serious doubts as to whether the ship could be saved. The main problem of sealing the damaged hull was solved by using wood and special underwater concrete patches 13 feet wide by 50 feet high bolted to the hull, making the ship watertight.

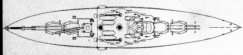

Back to War

On May 17, 1942, the WEST VIRGINIA was refloated and entered Dry Dock One. Temporary repairs were made to ready the vessel for its cruise to Puget Sound Navy Yard for modernization. The "Wee-Vee" proudly returned to service on September 14, 1944, in time for the invasion of the Philippines at Leyte Gulf in October of 1944.

Each day the crew of a battleship consumed 2100 pounds of meat, 4500 pounds of vegetables, 1050 pounds of bread, 375 pounds of coffee, 675 pounds of sugar and 150 gallons of milk.

Final Salute

Following the end of the war in the Pacific, WEST VIRGINIA was assigned to bring the troops home. It was called "Operation Magic Carpet." By mid-December, 1945, the "Wee Vee" had returned some 7,500 military personnel back to America.

Decommissioned on June 18, 1946, and placed in the Reserve Fleet, she was sold in 1961 for scrap.

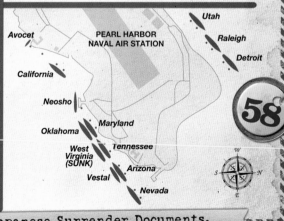

58

USS *Utah* (BB-31/AG-16)

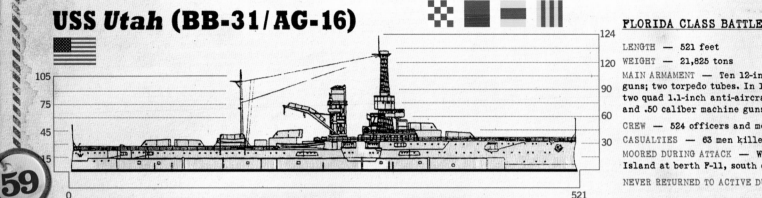

FLORIDA CLASS BATTLESHIP (1916)

LENGTH — 521 feet

WEIGHT — 21,825 tons

MAIN ARMAMENT — Ten 12-inch guns; 16 5-inch guns; two torpedo tubes. In 1941, eight 5-inch guns, two quad 1.1-inch anti-aircraft guns plus misc. and .50 caliber machine guns

CREW — 524 officers and men

CASUALTIES — 63 men killed

MOORED DURING ATTACK — West Side of Ford Island at berth F-11, south of the USS Raleigh.

NEVER RETURNED TO ACTIVE DUTY

History

The USS UTAH had its keel laying ceremony in Camden, New Jersey on March 9, 1909 and was commissioned on August 31, 1911 with the latest armament and firepower for its day. This illustrious "Dreadnaught Era" battleship enjoyed an eventful career and saw early action in revolution-torn Mexico in 1914 protecting American interests. In 1918, UTAH sailed to Europe after America entered World War One to protect convoys approaching the British Isles.

In 1934, UTAH was reclassified and converted to a dual-purpose ship serving the fleet as a mobile target and an auxiliary training vessel. With all armament removed, the ship was refitted with the latest in scientific and technological radio remote control advancements of its day. Most uniquely UTAH could now be completely controlled without any man-power aboard. Known as the "Robot Ship", it could steer, operate at varying speeds and maneuver like a ship in battle, all by remote control from another ship. In May 1941, UTAH sailed to Pearl Harbor where it joined the Pacific Fleet and continued its role as a mobile target and gunnery training ship until the day of the attack.

Not many ships at Pearl Harbor were older than the USS *Utah*. Commissioned in 1911, she served 21 years as a battleship BB-31 and then 10 years as AG-16, a training/target ship.

On December 7th, the USS UTAH was moored at a berth usually occupied by an aircraft carrier. It was the first ship attacked by Japanese planes and was quickly hit by two torpedoes. Immediately she began to roll over trapping 59 men inside. The senior officer gave the order to "Abandon Ship". Within seven minutes the UTAH had capsized. Only one man was rescued from the overturned hulk leaving 58 others still entombed within the ship to this day. 461 officers and men survived.

NOTES: JAPANESE COMMANDERS HAD ORDERED THEIR PILOTS TO IGNORE THE TRAINING SHIP, BUT EAGER PILOTS DROPPED TWO TORPEDOS ON THE UTAH.

Final Salute

Salvage engineers considered saving the UTAH. Their priority was to recover and save the combatant ships first. UTAH was a non-combatant ship and was therefore not considered for return to wartime service. UTAH's hulk had to be raised because it blocked a needed berth for aircraft carriers. By February 1944, the ship began to sink further into the mud and all salvage operations stopped. UTAH had been moved enough to clear the approach to an adjacent pier. To this day, the UTAH still remains at her berth F-11 on Ford Island's west side as a daily monument and final resting place for her crew still on eternal patrol.

UTAH at anchor in San Pedro, Calif. 1939

"The Utah was a target ship in those years before World War II. Twice a year we spread railroad ties over the decks, locked ourselves below, and let Navy planes plaster us with 100-pound water bombs. It was an eerie feeling, but we never had an accident" *Bob Kull "DOWN TO EARTH" column; Yakima Republic News; Yakima, Washington June 20, 1954*

Peter Tomich

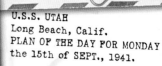

Utah's overturned hull lies at her berth.

Utah being righted with 17 giant cables

A Navy Hero's Medal Presented in Croatia

Anchored off the coast of Croatia, aboard the renowned U.S. aircraft carrier, USS ENTERPRISE (CVN-65) a little known story came to be...65 years later.

In 1942, the Medal of Honor, our nation's highest military honor, was posthumously awarded to Chief Watertender Peter Tomich, USN, for his "distinguished conduct in the line of his profession, and extraordinary courage and disregard of his own safety, during the attack on the Fleet in Pearl Harbor." He was an Austrian immigrant (now Bosnia) born in 1893 with the name of Petar Tonic and came to America with his cousin John in 1913.

Tomich served his entire adult life in the American military. By 1941, his rank was Chief Watertender and he served aboard the USS UTAH. He was known as one of the most competent sailors in his field. The UTAH was an old naval training ship. When young American pilots dropped "dummy bombs" from their aircraft--during practice drills--the UTAH was their target.

On December 7, 1941, the Japanese caught Pearl Harbor and the Pacific Fleet by surprise. 2,388 Americans lost their lives that day. Peter Tomich was one of them. It was thought the Japanese didn't consider the UTAH as a "high priority" with 8 fierce Battleships located on the "other" side of Ford Island. Yet the UTAH was one of the 1st ships to be hit. Tomich raced below to attempt to stabilize the ship and prevent an explosion. He insisted all other crew leave the engine room immediately. As Watertender, his job responsibility was tending to the many boilers in the ship's engine room. Tomich's dedication prevented the UTAH from exploding. But, as the ship overturned in a matter of minutes, listing at 40 degrees, Chief Tomich lost his life with 58 others.

Tomich was not married, nor did he have a family. But thanks to the persistence of Rear Admiral J. Robert Lunny and nine years of dedicated searching, the Navy was able to locate Tomich's next of kin for presentation of the Medal of Honor. Since 1974, the medal had been displayed at the Naval War College in Newport, Rhode Island.

On board the USS ENTERPRISE with full Navy regalia, Chief Watertender Peter Tomich's Medal of Honor was entrusted to his distant cousin, Lt. Col. Srecko Herzeg-Tonic. He retired from military service and is the grandson of Tomich's cousin, John Tonic, with whom he entered the United States in 1913.

U.S.S. UTAH
Long Beach, Calif.
PLAN OF THE DAY FOR MONDAY
the 15th of SEPT., 1941.

Duty Head of Dept. - Lt. Comdr. B:
CPO Duty Section - FIRST
Duty Watch - STARBOARD
Uniform of the Day - UNDRESS BLU
Duty Boat Crew No. 2; Standby No.

ROUTINE - Sea.

0530 Call all Idlere
0800 Turn to. Wash Down
0645 Up all hammocks
0700 Air Bedding
0730 Breakfast
0800 Quarters for muster and phy
0830 Sick Call
1130 Messcooks inspection
1200 Dinner
1500 Turn to. Continue ship's worl
1700 Emergency drill
1730 Supper
1830 Movies
2000 Pipe down

AVENGE December 7

These Colors WON'T RUN

Remember PEARL HARBOR

Suggested by ROD COOPER, Cincinnati Office

THE NAVY NEEDS SHIPS TO Avenge PEARL HARBOR

let's go

© BETHLEHEM STEEL COMPA

Keep 'Em FLYING

FOR VICTORY

V
...-

JOIN THE "V" CLUB OF AMERICA

BRITISH-AMERICAN AMBULANCE CORPS, N.Y.

Remember PEARL HARBOR

Remember PEARL HARBOR

★ REMEMBER ★

PEARL HARBOR

Remember PEARL HARBOR

61

AVENGE PEARL HARBOR

OUR BULLETS WILL DO IT

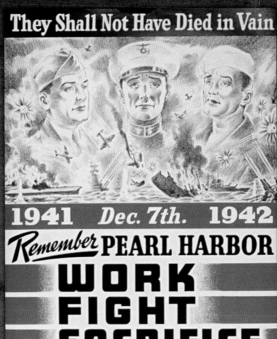

They Shall Not Have Died in Vain

1941 Dec. 7th. 1942

Remember PEARL HARBOR

WORK FIGHT SACRIFICE

Let's get it over with!

COME ON. C-H...DO MORE! THIS ISN'T PEACE-IT'S WAR!!

...*we here highly resolve that these dead shall not have died in vain*...

REMEMBER DEC. 7th!

REMEMBER PEARL HARBOR

Remember PEARL HARBOR

©EVER READY LABEL CORP. N Y

REMEMBER PEARL HARBOR DEC. 7th, 1941

REMEMBER PEARL HARBOR

SEALS for VICTORY

REMEMBER PEARL HARBOR

"Keep 'em Flying"

©1943 W. PELS EVER READY LABEL CORP. N. Y.

REMEMBER PEARL HARBOR

62

YEARS THAT FOLLOWED..

The devastating attack on Pearl Harbor, for all its tragedy, made the United States all the more aware that its western front was not the coast of California but, rather a group of islands some 2,000 miles to the southwest in the Pacific Ocean. The people of Hawaii had long been preparing for war. Evacuation drills had been ongoing for a year. Islanders responded almost immediately as teams of civilian doctors, nurses and volunteers rushed to military and civilian hospitals and casualty centers.

Hawaii was now: barbed wire beaches, gas alarm signs, air raid shelters, and victory gardens. Rationing was in effect due to shortages of consumer goods from the states. Tens of thousands of volunteers and war workers poured into the Islands from the mainland to assist in the salvage of the damaged ships, the repair of broken defenses and the building of new ones.

AIR RAID PRECAUTIONS MANUAL

Mr. and Mrs. Gordon from Waikiki built a home-made bomb shelter from a trench with a heavy cover, piled high with earth. December 1941.

V ...—

NAME Jane L Winne   NO. 892
ADDRESS Punahou School
ASSIGNED TO Castle Memorial . University of Hawaii
District D   No. 21
EVACUATION CENTER.

HAS TO PROCEED ON THE STREETS
DURING AN EVACUATION EMERGENCY.

PASS BEARER

APPROVED BY _____
PROVOST MARSHAL

DATE: 3 0 MAY 1942

TOP PHOTO: As the army began to take over the Islands after the attack, all government buildings became military offices. Beaches and airports were strung with barbed wire, as was Iolani Palace in early 1942. BOTTOM PHOTO: Barbed wire was strung across Waikiki Beach near the Royal Hawaiian Hotel, which served as a place for military staff to enjoy a break from wartime duties.

PREPARED UNDER THE DIRECTION OF THE
COMMANDING GENERAL
HAWAIIAN DEPARTMENT

MARTIAL LAW DECLARED; EATHS ARE MOUNTING

8 PAGES—HONOLULU, TERRITORY OF HAWAII, U.S.A., SUNDAY, DECEMBER 7, 1941—8 PAGES   ★★★ PRICE FIVE CENTS

ring that a full scale invasion was imminent, vernor Poindexter issued a proclamation placing e Islands under martial law, known as the M-Day t. It meant that the military was in complete ntrol of the courts. The newspapers, telephones, dio and even the mail would be censored. Strict rfews and nightly blackouts were heavily enforced. e entire civilian population over six years of age d to be fingerprinted and carry ID cards at all times.

Beretania Street, Honolulu
August 1942

U.S. ARMY

Honolulu Star-Bulletin - December 7, 1941 - 1st EXTRA

CIVILIANS ORDERED OFF STREETS

The army has ordered that all civilians stay off the streets and highways and not use telephones. Evidence that the Japanese attack has registered some hits was shown by three billowing pillars of smoke in the Pearl Harbor and Hickam field area. All U.S. Navy personnel and civilian defense workers, with the exception of women, have been ordered to duty at Pearl Harbor.

The Pearl Harbor highway was immediately a mass of racing cars. A trickling stream of injured people began pouring into the city emergency hospital a few minutes after the bombardment started. Thousands of telephone calls almost swamped the Mutual Telephone Co., which put extra operators on duty. At the Star-Bulletin office the phone calls deluged the single operator and it was impossible for this newspaper, for some time, to handle the flood of calls. Here also an emergency operator was called.

The streets were continually filled with soldiers and sailors. The roads became a constant procession of trucks and tanks, jeeps with trailers and busloads of civilian workers all going about the business of war. Hawaii performed a remarkable role as the giant staging base and supply center for all the Pacific theaters of the World War Two.

Jan. 42

dren from the Royal School in Honolulu display temporary gency masks. The army provided masks for the 700 students cost of 4 cents each.

The Ala Moana Rifle Range in Honolulu held gas attack drills. Three female employees from the Honolulu Police Department practice putting on gas masks at the range. The women complained of stinging eyes and dizziness from the effects of the simulated gas attacks.

JAPANESE

Racial Hatred Has Gone Too Far...

JAPANESE AMERICANS.... THE ENEMY?

When the last Japanese plane left the scene of carnage on that fateful Sunday morning of December 7th, the lives of Americans of Japanese Ancestry (AJAs) in Hawaii and especially those on the mainland would undergo a dramatic and degrading change. Within hours after the attack martial law was declared in Hawaii. It meant that the military was in complete control of the courts. Any person of Japanese descent would have their lives unalterably changed, affecting generations to come.

TRANSIT

WRA Camp Populations:

Manzanar, California	10,000
Tule Lake, California	16,000
Poston, Arizona (3 units)	20,000
Gila River, Ariz. (2 units)	15,000
Minidoka, Idaho	10,000
Topaz, Utah	10,000
Granada, Colorado	8,000
Heart Mountain, Wyoming	12,000
Jerome, Arkansas	10,000
Rohwer, Arkansas	10,000

SHIPPING No. _____

SIGNATURE: _____

Hawaii Japs Are Head

WASHINGTON · OREGON · IDAHO · Minido · Tule Lake · NEVADA · U · Topaz · MO. · CALIFORNIA · Manzanar · LEUPP · ARIZO · Poston · Gila Riv

Evicted Japs Banished to Camps

Baltimore News Daily   EDITORIALS

ALL MEN ARE NOT CREATED EQUAL

The people of the Territory of Hawaii had been practicing routine evacuation plans during 1940 and 1941. But no one could have anticipated the shock and devastation that ensued on the morning of Dec. 7, 1941. The reaction to the Japanese planned attack was instantaneous. A militaristic and patriotic pride swept over the country. The United States had one thing in mind--avenge the Japanese attack. Retaliation became the theme that held the United States together until the war was over. Americans stood shoulder to shoulder pursuing this common goal and everyone took part. Yet along with this fervor came war hysteria and fear. Everyone feared that the Japanese would bomb the United States again. Families in Oahu were terrified that the Japanese would again attack Hawaiian soil. Many frightened mothers and children who lived near Pearl Harbor slept hidden in sugar cane fields for weeks after the attack. Public hysteria was at an all time high. The government's heightened suspicion of Japanese espionage and sabotage within the United States became paramount. Upholding the Declaration of Independence's statement that "all men are created equal" was simply not possible.

WAR RELOCATION AUTHORITY

◆ Relocation Center

■ Isolation Center

ARMY ORD

Imagine: being forced to sell your home, business and personal property for a few cents on the dollar.

Issei 一世 1st generation Japanese who immigrated to the United States.

Nisei 二世 The 2nd generation children born in the United States from Japanese parents who immigrated from Japan.

In the waning days of

Mainland

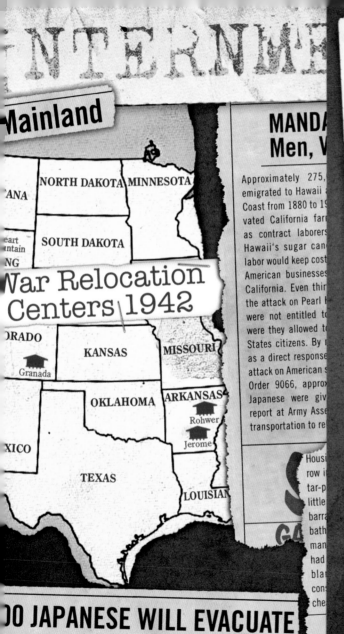

War Relocation Centers 1942

(States shown: NORTH DAKOTA, MINNESOTA, SOUTH DAKOTA, KANSAS, MISSOURI, OKLAHOMA, ARKANSAS, TEXAS, LOUISIAN..., COLORADO, ...XICO; camp markers at Granada, Rohwer, Jerome)

MANDA... Men, W...

Approximately 275,... emigrated to Hawaii a... Coast from 1880 to 1... vated California farr... as contract laborers... Hawaii's sugar can... labor would keep cost... American businesses... California. Even thir... the attack on Pearl H... were not entitled t... were they allowed t... States citizens. By... as a direct response... attack on American s... Order 9066, approx... Japanese were giv... report at Army Asse... transportation to re...

Hous... row i... tar-p... little... barra... bath... man... had... bla... cons... che...

O JAPANESE WILL EVACUATE

Camp "C," Block 2,
43rd Quarter
Puallup, Wash.
May 10, 1942

Dear Miss Evanson and
Pupils,

After 2 days of packing
and fixing our new home
in Puallup I wish to
say, "hello" in as short
way. Now to begin
with our room, we
have one room shared
among 7 pupils and
the walls too are full of
holes and cracks in which
cold and chill air
struck us in a funny
way that I cold could
not sleep at all last
night. We had so little
to to eat that after

reaching our room I ate a
sandwich and some
crackers. Our beds are
on loose by the U. S. Army
and our mattress is a
cloth bag strawed by hay.
Now is a nice place
to end my letter so
"good bye" until next time
and please write to me,
all.

Your Seattle
evacuee

Miss Evanson loved her students at the George Washington Junior High School in Seattle, Washington. Many of these children were Japanese-Americans. After Pearl Harbor was attacked, many were interned with their families at Camp Harmony, California. Miss Evanson encouraged these students to write her during their time there, providing a rare glimpse into the drastic changes the children endured living in prison camps.

"Go For Broke"

After the attack on Pearl Harbor, second generation Nisei were denied from serving in the military because of their presumed lack of loyalty to the United States. In early 1943, the Hawaiian War Department announced that 1,500 AJA (American's of Japanese Ancestry) volunteers would be allowed to enlist in the Army. Nearly 10,000 answered the call, but only about 2,600 would be selected. From September 1943 to May 1944 they fought many fierce battles in Italy earning the nickname, "The Purple Heart Battalion." On June 10, 1944, the 100th Battalion would join with fellow AJA soldiers from the mainland as part of the 442nd Regimental Combat Team. The men chose "Go For Broke!" as their motto, an island expression meaning "Shoot The Works!" Winning more than 9,000 citations, the 100th/442nd was the most decorated unit in the history of the United States military.

2nd Lts. Kaichi and Yoshida from the 442nd in Italy.

On the HOME FRONT

On the eve of December 7, 1941, America was still at peace. It abruptly ended the next morning in the waters of Pearl Harbor. For most Americans the chilling impact of war was both shocking and frightening, almost unbelievable. People were angry and determined for revenge against Japan.

War meant that every aspect of life in America would change profoundly for the duration. New cars and new homes, appliances such as stoves and refrigerators, radios and record players, plus a myriad of commodities and materials essential to war production would no longer be available.

War meant sacrifices at home and within the very hearts of families as loved ones went off to war. Air raid drills with blaring sirens, blackouts, rationing of consumer goods and long lines became a part of everyday life.

War meant people on the move. Millions across the land left their homes and farms to work in distant defense plants and shipyards. Eventually more than 12 million men and women would serve in the Armed Forces. The shortage of men in the work force opened opportunities for nearly 6 million women to work and contribute to the war effort.

War meant Civil Defense, blood banks, the Red Cross, victory gardens, war bond drives and scrap metal drives. Even school kids around the country knocked on doors, searched in backyards, alleys and vacant lots looking for rubber, tin cans and other metals.

It would be nearly four long years before life in America would return to the peace it knew on the eve of December 7, 1941.

KEEP 'EM FLYING

V FOR VICTORY

MOTHERS OF WORLD WAR II

WE CAN...
WE WILL..
WE MUST !
..Franklin D. Roosevelt

BUY U.S. WAR SAVINGS BONDS & STAMPS NOW

WIN THE WAR 3¢ UNITED STATES POSTAGE

UNITED STATES POSTAGE

Women at War

Buy WAR BONDS

We Can Do It!

W.A.S.P.

FOR VICTORY

Spend Less to Lend More to Your Country

Our fighting men are risking their very lives to win. The least we at home can do is to lend our money to help meet the costs of war and to avoid the dangers of inflation. Series E War Bonds are issued in $25, $50, $100, $500, and $1,000 denominations, which cost, respectively, $18.75, $37.50, $75, $375, and $750.

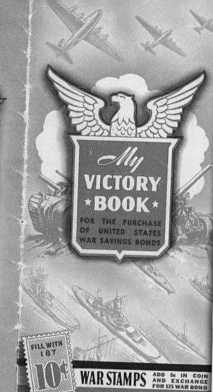

My **VICTORY BOOK**

FOR THE PURCHASE OF UNITED STATES WAR SAVINGS BONDS

FILL WITH 187

10¢

WAR STAMPS

ADD 5¢ IN COIN AND EXCHANGE FOR $25 WAR BOND

To Have and to Hold!

WAR BONDS

AKE THIS PLEDGE:
pay no more than top legal prices
accept no rationed goods
ithout giving up ration stamps

VICTORY GARDENS

MISCELLANEOUS PUBLICATION NO. 483

U.S. DEPARTMENT OF AGRICULTURE

GROW YOUR OWN *Be sure!*

GARDEN V VICTORY

YOUR VICTORY GARDEN
counts more than ever!

Save!

WASTE PAPER AND HELP WIN THE WAR

Buy!
UNITED STATES SAVINGS DEFENSE BONDS AND STAMPS

Made in U
THE DIAMOND MA

68

YOU AND YOUR FUEL OIL RATION

Gas, food and merchandise were in very short supply during the war and allocating ration books with stamps made sure everyone would have their small but equal share.

2

WAR RATION BOOKS

PROPERTY OF

NAME _____

ADDRESS _____

CITY _____

3 Every man, woman and child was given a monthly ration book, which in turn helped keep the demand low for food and goods. Businesses determined which stamps to use each week based on the stamp's letter. People still had to pay money for these items, but stamps were essential. Rationing stamps were good for cheese, canned foods, butter, meat, oil, even shoes. Many things became almost impossible to buy such as coffee and sugar.

69

1 A complex distribution system was set up by the government's Office of P Administration (OPA) authorizing war rationing. Americans received a bool rationing stamps every month for purchasing all types of goods. Very items could be bought without these stamps.

UNITED STATES OF AMERICA

War Ration Book One

WARNING

1 Punishments ranging as high as *Ten Years' Imprisonment* or $10,000 *Fine, or Both,* may be imposed under United States Statutes for violations thereof arising out of infractions of Rationing Orders and Regulations.

2 This book must be transferred. It must be held and used only by or on behalf of the person to whom it has been issued, and anyone presenting it thereby represents to the Office of Price Administration, an agency of the United States Government, that it is being so held and so used. For any misuse of this book it may be taken from the holder by the Office of Price Administration.

No. 590760 -339

OFFICE OF PRICE ADMINISTRATION
OFFICIAL BUSINESS

PENALTY FOR PRIVATE USE TO AVOID
PAYMENT OF POSTAGE. $300

POSTMASTER:–DO NOT FORWARD
IF UNDELIVERED RETURN TO

OPA MAIL CENTER
NEW YORK, N. Y.

4 Coupon rationing authorized equal shares for good like coffee, shoes and sugar, whereas point ration allowed purchases for items such as meats, fats, cheese, canned meat and canned milk.

268/590 AK UNITED STATES OF AMERICA
OFFICE OF PRICE ADMINISTRATION

WAR RATION BOOK TWO

IDENTIFICATION

JoAnn Smith
(Name of person to whom book is issued)

320 Winder Ave
(Street number or rural route)

Tracy _____ Calif _____
(City or post office) (State) (Age) (Sex)

ISSUED BY LOCAL BOARD No. 89-11-4 Tw San Joaquin Calif.
(County) (State)

255 Central Ave _____ Tracy
(Street address of local board) (City)

_____
(Signature of issuing officer)

SIGNATURE Jo Ann Smith
(To be signed by the person to whom this book is issued. If such person is unable to sign be...

STUB _____ UNITED STATES OF AMERICA
OFFICE OF PRICE ADMINISTRATION _____ STUB

WAR RATION BOOK No. 3· IDENTIFICATION STUB
AFTER COMPLETING THIS APPLICATION, TEAR OFF THIS STUB AND BE SURE
TO KEEP IT UNTIL YOU GET YOUR WAR RATION BOOK No. 3

Tear Off Here _____ No. 177642 A _____ Tear Off Here

STATES OF AMERICA
PRICE ADMINISTRATION

EL OIL RATION
Consumer Coupons
ve-Gallon Coupons)

OFFICE OF
PRICE ADM.
R-123

is number in ink on each the
After each 5 or 10 check
number for accuracy.

46833   L8   46833

CT-1   1943   Date   SEP 30 1944
expires
upons
ed to Mary E Hicks

O.P.A. Form No. R-306

Serial No. C 45237883

UNITED STATES OF AMERICA
OFFICE OF PRICE ADMINISTRATION
SUGAR PURCHASE CERTIFICATE

Not Valid Before 8/19

TRIPLICATE

THIS IS TO CERTIFY THAT:

Name: Mrs W. A. Hicks   Address:

City: Dexter   County: Jefferson   State: New York

is authorized to accept delivery of
Thirty-One   pounds of
pursuant to Rationing Order No. 3 (Sugar Rationing Regulations) of, and   not to exceed the maximum price establi
the Office of Price Administration.

Date:

Local Rationing Board No. 22-0-1   By:

Jefferson N Y
State

To Be Ret

RATION
BOOK HOLDER

M 8

M 5

The military and wartime efforts took precedence over
the needs of American civilians who were challenged
by the new experience of having to do with less, even
if they had money for more.

SPARE SPARE SPARE SPARE

M

UNITED STATES OF AMERICA
OFFICE OF PRICE ADMINISTRATION

SUGAR RATION BOOK

NAME
ADDRESS NUMBER AND STREET

Rationing in
World War II

5

Wartime production took priority over consumer goods. Factories
converted to manufacturing items that were needed strictly for the war
effort. Rubber was a commodity that America previously purchased
from the Dutch East Indies, which was now under Japanese rule.
Rubber was completely unavailable. Donating rubber for recycling
became America's obsession, as it was the wartime's most valuable
resource. Businesses and factories that once made cars or popular
metal toys for children now manufactured metal shells for ammunition
as well as tanks, jeeps and trucks. Gasoline was rationed. Sugar was
nearly impossible to buy. Coca-Cola reduced production by 50% as
sugar was used to make gun powder, which meant candy and gum
were also unavailable. Womens much-beloved silk stockings became
impossible to find. Rationing was a challenging time, to say the least.

What Things Cost in Hawaii in 1942

Steak	50¢ per pound
Prime Rib	37¢ per pound
Rump Roast	37¢ per pound
Hamburger	27¢ per pound
Fish: pond mullet	50¢ per pound
Island eggs large	85¢ dozen
Rice	9¢ per pound
Onion	9¢ per pound
Sugar	7 5¢ per pound
Potatoes	6¢ per pound
Lemons	35¢ dozen
Cheese	39¢ per pound
Bananas	5¢ per pound
Papayas	4¢ per pound
Pineapples	3¢ per pound

H 2

H 1

Go
by
bus

RATION
STAMP NO.
1

RATION
STAMP NO.
2

RATION
STAMP NO.
5

RATION
STAMP NO.
6

RATION
STAMP NO.
9

RATION
STAMP NO.
10

7

Unless otherwise announced, the Ration Week was from
Saturday midnight to the following Saturday midnight.

12   12   12

A   A   A   A
Mileage   Mileage   Mileage   Mileage
Ration   Ration   Ration   Ration

FOLD

Go
by
bus

RATION
STAMP NO.
21

RATION
STAMP NO.
22

RATION
STAMP NO.
25

RATION
STAMP NO.
26

UNITED STATES OF AMERICA
OFFICE OF PRICE ADMINISTRATION

WAR RATION BOOK No. 3   Void if altered

606513   C

O.P.A.
NOT
VALID
WITHOUT
STAMP

Identification of person to whom issued: PRINT IN FULL

Minnie   C   Beck
(First name)   (Middle name)   (Last name)

Street number or rural route Mc Bride Ave

City or post office Clinton   State New York

AGE	SEX	WEIGHT	HEIGHT	OCCUPATION
46		150 Lbs.	5 Ft. 8 In.	Bookkeeper

SIGNATURE Minnie C. Beck

A

BASIC MILEAGE RATION

UNITED STATES OF AMERICA
OFFICE OF PRICE ADMINISTRATION   No 638594 A K

Form OPA R-525B   NAME OF REGISTERED OWNER

VEHICLE LICENSE NO.

STATE OF REGISTRATION:

COMPLETE ADDRESS:

C Beck

Mc Bride Ave

YEAR MODEL: 1938

MAKE:

Go
by
bus

RATION
STAMP NO.
29

RATION
STAMP NO.
30

RATION
STAMP NO.
33

RATION
STAMP NO.
34

70

RATION
STAMP NO.
37

The
UNITED STATES
ARMY

THEN ~ NOW ~ FOREVER

During the war, artists, academics and filmmakers, some of whom received no pay at all, worked to create many different patriotic themes to give a voice to our nation's resolve. They used pamphlets, movies, radio, books, magazines and animation. But the American propaganda posters of World War Two, defined by their stunning visual and verbal message, effectively communicated the nation's wartime effort to its public. Over 200,000 different posters were printed during this time.

OER THE RAMPARTS WE WATCH

71

UNITED STATES
ARMY AIR FORCES

"SUB SPOTTED—
LET 'EM HAVE IT!"

LEND A HAND—

BUY WAR BONDS

WOMAN'S PLACE IN W
The Army of the United State
has 239 kinds of jobs for wome
THE WOMEN'S ARMY CO

WANTS

Some posters were motivational, some spoke to preserving our freedom and others addressed what Americans could do to support the war effort. Some posters were strictly informational and some were more subtle. But in all, they spread an idea. These powerful, familiar images and phrases spoke to what our country was fighting for. Their goal: to stimulate and encourage the American population to support and sustain the war effort that would ultimately lead to victory over our enemies in the Pacific and European fronts.

BUY A SHARE IN AMERICA

DEFENSE SAVINGS BONDS AND STAMPS

WANT YOU

the U.S. ARMY
ENLIST NOW

Longing won't bring him back sooner...
GET A WAR JOB!
SEE YOUR U. S. EMPLOYMENT SERVICE
WAR MANPOWER COMMISSION

Man the GUNS
Join the NAVY

"you buy 'em we'll fly 'em!"

DEFENSE BONDS STAMPS

72

PRESIDENT ROOSEVELT IS DEAD

Dies Suddenly at Warm Springs, Georgia

Truman Sworn In

April 12, 1945 - Franklin Delano Roosevelt, President of the United States died suddenly at 4:35 p.m. today, in Warm Springs, Georgia. He was 63 years old.

The President died from a cerebral hemorrhage, just passed the 83rd day of his fourth term and was moving ever-closer to war's end with Japan and Germany.

Vice-President Truman was sworn in as the 32nd President of the United States in a one minute ceremony, less than two hours after the President's death was announced. President Truman vowed to continue in the same vain as Roosevelt to continue fighting the war in the East and West.

Mrs. Eleanor Roosevelt sent word by telegraph to her four sons serving in the military. She said: "He did his job to the end as he would want you to do. Bless you all and all our love. Mother."

Death Shocks The World

In Peace and in war, President Franklin Roosevelt

JAPAN'S ADMIRAL YAMAMOTO KILLED IN ACTION 1943

Admiral Isoruku Yamamoto was killed April 18, 1943, when his plane was downed near Bougainville in the North Solomon Islands and crashed into the jungle. On April 14, 1943, U.S. Magic Code Breakers intercepted specific intelligence from the Japanese Navy that provided Admiral Yamamoto's whereabouts on April 14. Therefore, by order of the President, Navy Secretary Frank Knox and Admiral Nimitz, "Operation Vengeance" was born and specifically targeted Yamamoto. Admiral Halsey, Commander of the South Pacific Forces took charge as his forces were nearest to the Solomon Islands. Eighteen P-38 Lightnings from Squadron 339 and Fighter Group 347 went after the three Japanese bomber planes known as "Betty's", as well as a grouping of "ZEROs". Two of the three "BETTYs" were shot down. The plane that carried Yamamoto crashed into the jungle and the other into the ocean. Four of the U.S. squadron pilots were given credit for bringing down Yamamoto and the 16 returning pilots received the Navy Cross.

山本五十六

戦死

*Admiral Yamamoto dies in battle

"THESE PROCEEDINGS ARE CLOSED"

--General Douglas MacArthur-- stated after the Surrender Instrument was signed by the Japanese on the Battleship Missouri in Tokyo Bay on September 2, 1945.

When the first bombs fell on Pearl Harbor the twenty-three years and twenty-six days of peace between the ending of World War One and the Sunday morning of December 7, 1941, came to a sobering end for America. The following day the United States declared war against the Empire of Japan. That same day Japanese forces attacked the Philippines, Hong Kong, Guam, Wake Island, Borneo and Malaya. Three days later Germany and Italy, allies of Japan, declared war against the United States. That same day, Congress followed up with a unanimous vote "that a state of war now exists against Germany and Italy." What followed were turbulent and destructive years between the great powers of the world. Nations representing half of the world's population were now involved in what history would remember as World War Two.

America remained at war for nearly four years. It was a time when American men and women answered the call to arms to serve their country in the military or on the home front in factories and shipyards. At home, the United States became a formidable military juggernaut, performing miracles with its industrial output of aircraft production and ship building. It was a time of great sacrifice and courage.

The war which began at Pearl Harbor on December 7, 1941, ended on August 15, 1945, when President Harry S. Truman broadcast over the radio to America and her allies the much anticipated news that Japan had accepted the terms of unconditional surrender. A peace treaty was signed at Tokyo Bay September 2, 1945, aboard the mighty USS *Missouri*. Present in the harbor was the 5 battle-starred USS *West Virginia* which witnessed and endured the

In the United States, crowds gathered everywhere with people yelling and cheering over the news that the war had ended. They danced and sang in the streets. Strangers embraced and kissed while others wept with joy. Church bells rang, cars honked, factory whistles blew while sirens screamed and ships' foghorns bellowed. People flocked to their churches and synagogues to pray and give thanks. It was a day when all freedom-loving people of the world rejoiced in peace.

The guns were silent. A horrible tragedy had ended. Overjoyed with the news of Japan's surrender, millions of war-weary men and women in uniform knew they would be going home at last. It would be a different world to greet them but the long, hard-fought war that began for America on December 7, 1941, was finally over.

Now was a time for peace and remembrance.

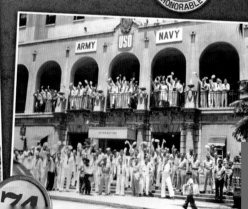

Remember
PEARL HARBOR

U.S.S. ARIZONA
MEMORIAL
BB-39

Out of the ashes of defeat came the resilience of a people tested by war and resolved to preserve peace. This is what the Pearl Harbor experience is all about.

The USS *Arizona* Memorial was built with a low center and higher ends for architectural, structural and aesthetic reasons. The U.S. Navy decided that the Memorial should in no way touch the ship as it is the final resting place for 1,177 members of the *Arizona's* crew. Therefore, Honolulu architect Alfred Preis designed a memorial which would span the ship like a suspension bridge but not touch the ship. The Memorial rests on pillars that were dug into the harbor floor on both sides of the ship so the majority of its weight was positioned at both ends.

The USS ARIZONA Memorial was dedicated on Memorial Day 1962 and pays tribute to all who lost their lives as a result of the Japanese attack on the island of Oahu on December 7, 1941.

People come to the USS ARIZONA Memorial to remember a day of war in a time of peace.

FLAGPOLE LOCATION

The position of the Memorial over the ship was partly influenced by the location of the flagpole at the base of the ship's rear mast. In March of 1950, Admiral Arthur Radford, Commander in Chief of the Pacific Fleet, ordered the flag to be flown over the *Arizona*.

Oil still seeps from the rusting USS ARIZONA at a rate of approximately 1 gallon per day. When the ARIZONA was sunk, there was an estimated 1.4 million gallons of oil onboard. The droplets of oil, known as "Black Tears," are a symbol to the loss of life and those whose remains are still entombed.

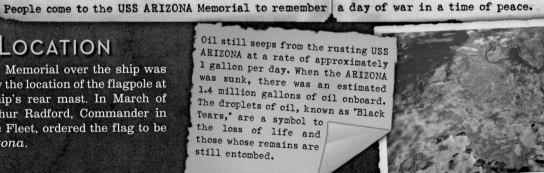

An aerial view of the Memorial poignantly straddling the rusted footprint of a sunken *Arizona* below.

Arizona as it sits on the bottom of Pearl Harbor

The low center of the Memorial can be interpreted to express initial defeat, while the gradual sweep of its higher ends can symbolize ultimate victory.

There were 1,177 USS Arizona crewmen who were killed as a result of the Pearl Harbor attack. The majority are still entombed within the ship. More than 200 remains were recovered, many of which could not be identified.

THE PACIFIC WAR MEMORIAL COMMISSION
proudly presents **ELVIS PRESLEY**
IN PERSON
★ WITH ALL-STAR CAST ★
AT BLOCH ARENA   PEARL HARBOR
Saturday, March 25th, 1961   8:30 p.m.
Doors Open 7:15

MAIN FLOOR
1 4
$100 SECTION

BUILDING THE MEMORIAL

Construction began in 1960 after the Pacific War Memorial Commission raised over $250,000 during the two-year period. The cost of the Memorial was over $500,000 and the remaining $250,000 was allocated by the Hawaii Legislature and U.S. Congress.

A benefit concert held at Pearl Harbor's Bloch Arena by Elvis Presley on March 25, 1961, raised more than $64,000. Four thousand frenzied fans paid either $3.00, $3.50, $5.00 or $10 per ticket with 300 ring side seats available for a whopping $100. Also, Ralph Edwards of the television program, "This Is Your Life," held a special broadcast and raised $95,000 in donations.

A white marble wall is enclosed within the Memorial, known as the Shrine Room. On this wall are inscribed the names of the USS ARIZONA crew members who were killed as a result of the attack on December 7, 1941.

Significant Quotes...

"In view of the great possibility of being compelled to go to war against the United States, Great Britain and the Netherlands in the cause of self-existence and self-defense, Japan has decided to complete various operational preparations within the first ten days of December."

--Osami Nagano, Chief of the Naval General Staff
By Imperial Order to Admiral Yamamoto, Commander in Chief of the Combined Fleet
Navy Order No. 1 - November 5, 1941

66 I headed for my battle station down on 3rd deck at the forward air compressors. When I got there there was this loud explosion which I later learned was from torpedoes which blew a 157 ft. hole in the hull. The ship started to capsize and we counter flooded as best we could then headed for topside to keep from drowning. It was 3 steps forward and 2 steps back but I made it to the fo'c'sle (forecastle) and crawled under one of the 16-inch gun turrets to keep from getting machine gunned. 99

--James D. Hunter, USS *West Virginia*

皇国ノ興廃繋リテ此ノ征戦二在リ
粉骨砕身各員其ノ任ヲ　完ウセヨ

66 **The fate of the Empire rests in this operation. All personnel do your duty even it means broken bodies and bones crushed to dust.** 99

--Sent by telegram from Naval Head Quarters in Tokyo to Admiral Yamamoto at 2 a.m. December 6.

--Ensign Perry L. Teaff U.S.N., Pilot of Scouting Squadron Six-2
U.S.S. Enterprise Action Report December 7, 1941

"AT 8:05 I APPROACHED BARBERS POINT FROM THE NORTHWEST. WE OBSERVED PLANES ATTACKING EWA FIELD... A JAPANESE FIGHTER PLANE PULLED UP IN A WING OVER AND MADE AN ATTACK ON ME. I ASSUMED IT WAS ONE OF OUR ARMY PLANES SINCE I HAD NOT YET REALIZED WHAT WAS HAPPENING...AT ABOUT 75 FEET HE OPENED FIRE. NO BULLETS HIT THE RADIOMAN OR MYSELF BUT THEY WERE LIBERALLY SPRINKLED THROUGH PARTS OF THE PLANE. THEY APPEARED TO BE .30 CALIBER SINCE SOME OF THEM GLANCED OFF THE WING SURFACE. THE FIGHTER TURNED AND MADE ANOTHER ATTACK. I TURNED TO THE RIGHT AS HE APPROACHED AND MY REAR SEAT MAN FIRED A SHORT BURST."

Ensign Teaff took off in his aircraft accompanied with Scouting Squadron 1 after 12:30 p.m. lookir for the Japanese aircraft carriers north of Oahu. But due to a Japanese bullet lodged in the engine, oil temperatures rose to 100° and was forced to turn around. They landed safely at Ford Island.

"We had come into Pearl on Friday and were due for an inspection on Monday, so all our watertight bulkheads were open and our ammunition was locked up. I was near my bunk on the second deck with some of my shipmates deciding where to go on liberty. When the first torpedo struck we were all knocked down. We got up and ran to our battle stations on the fifth deck and I remember passing my brother Arthur on the third deck. Other hits came in rapid succession when the power went off and it was pitch black. The smell of cordite powder was overpowering. We had to abandon the boiler room as it was flooding rapidly and the ship began to roll over. We were climbing to the third deck looking for a way out when Chief Watertender Francis D. Day called down to anyone who could hear that he had a porthole open on the starboard side. With water closing over the porthole he managed to push me and another 14 men through before the ship completely rolled over. But it was too late for him, he never made it out. That evening I learned that my brother Arthur didn't make it either."

-- John D. Grand Pre
U.S.S. *Oklahoma* BB-36

"The Carrier Striking Task Force will proceed to the Hawaiian Area with utmost secrecy and, at the outbreak of the war, will launch a resolute surprise attack on and deal a fatal blow to the enemy fleet in the Hawaiian Area."

--Chuichi Nagumo, Commander of the Carrier Striking Task Force, November 23, 1941

66 This means war! 99

--President Franklin Delano Roosevelt
After reading the decoded and translated 13-part memorandum from the Japanese Government to the State Department December 6, 1941 late afternoon or early evening.

66 We felt the ship shake from the explosion of the first aerial torpedo which penetrated the skin of the ship.... 'Man your general quarters stations' was passed on the loudspeaker system. I grabbed the first pair of shoes I saw, my new white moccasins and ran to Main Control... I must have gotten to my station, Main Control, in less than a minute...There was not time to say much of anything. I remember Yeoman Ross... asking me, "What is this?" I replied, "This is it." Everyone present knew what these words meant. 99

--Werner K. Bauer, U.S.S. *West Virginia* December 9, 1941

- ACTION REPORT -

"AT 0825, I WAS APPROACHING BARBERS POINT FROM THE SOUTH AT 1500 FEET ALTITUDE WHEN I NOTICED NUMEROUS SHELL SPLASHES IN THE WATER BY THE ENTRANCE TO PEARL HARBOR. I THEN LOOKED FOR THE SOURCE. I COULD SEE ONE CRUISER AND THREE DESTROYERS ABOUT THREE MILES OFF THE ENTRANCE BUT THEY WERE NOT FIRING. UPON LOOKING UPWARDS I SAW NUMEROUS ANTI-AIRCRAFT BURSTS ABOVE PEARL HARBOR... SMOKE WAS RISING FROM WHAT TURNED OUT TO BE THE USS ARIZONA... I HAD SEEN NO ENEMY PLANES AS YET, BUT WAS VERY SHORTLY ATTACKED BY TWO JAPANESE FIGHTERS AS WE HEADED TOWARDS PEARL HARBOR. AS WE WENT DOWN TO 1000 FEET HEADED TOWARDS PEARL HARBOR THE ABOVE ENEMY PLANES WERE JOINED BY ABOUT FOUR OTHERS. DURING THIS TIME, MY PLANE WAS UNDER FIRE FROM 3 - 5 ENEMY PLANES. MY GUNNER REPORTED THAT HE HAD BEEN HIT FOLLOWED BY A REPORT THAT HE HAD HIT AN ENEMY PLANE. ALL OF HIS AMMUNITION WAS EXPENDED AND HE HAD BEEN HIT AGAIN. I LOOKED AFT AND SAW A JAPANESE PLANE ON FIRE SLOWLY LOSING SPEED AND ALTITUDE BUT DID NOT ACTUALLY SEE HIM STRIKE THE GROUND. AT THIS TIME I WAS ABLE TO GET IN TWO SHORT BURSTS FROM MY FIXED GUNS AS ONE ENEMY AIRCRAFT PULLED AHEAD."

--Lieutenant C. E. Dickinson, Jr.
U.S.N., Pilot of Scouting Squadron Six-4
U.S.S. *Enterprise*

"I was shocked to see the row of battleships in front of my eyes... I didn't have time to say "ready", so I just said "fire". The navigator in the back pulled the release lever. The plane lightened with the sound of the torpedo being released. I kept flying low and flew right through, just above the ship... I asked my observer, 'Is the torpedo going all right?'... Soon he said, 'It hit it'... My torpedo hit the mark. I saw two water columns go up and go down...But then I realized we're being attacked from behind...I was avoiding bullets by swinging my plane from right to left. I felt frightened for the time and thought my duty was finished. I headed back to the meeting place."

--Japanese Pilot Lieutenant Goto
December 7, 1941

Dickinson's SB Dauntless caught fire and his controls were shot away leaving he and his gunner, William C. Miller, no choice but to jump. Dickinson parachuted to safety near Ewa Field and made his way back to Ford Island. Williams, however was seriously wounded, shot twice by a Japanese "ZERO" and was killed before or after his plane crashed. Dickinson saw much more combat in the Pacific, as well as the Battle of Midway. He earned 3 Navy Crosses by the end of the war.

> I awakened about 0730 on the morning of December 7, dressed, and walked into the wardroom in preparation for breakfast. As I sat down, over the announcing system came the word, "Japanese planes are attacking Ford Island. All hands to General Quarters." Immediately I ran up to the main deck... As I reached the main deck I was jarred by a tremendous explosion which seemed to lift the ship several feet... At this time I saw at least seven torpedo planes which had apparently just passed over the *Helena* dropping torpedos aimed at the row of battleships moored across from us. All had big red discs on their wings, and my estimate of their altitude when they dropped their torpedos was from 50 to 75 feet above the water.

--Ensign MILLER, U.S.N. U.S.S. *Helena* Damage Report

"BRILLIANTLY EXECUTED MILITARY MANEUVER"...

--Admiral Kimmel, Commander of the Pacific Fleet,
To the congressional committee investigating Pearl Harbor

> It is natural that I should bear entire responsibility for the war in general, and, needless to say, I am prepared to do so... now that the war has been lost, it is... necessary that I be judged so that time can be clarified and the future peace of the world be assured.

--Prime Minister Hideki Tojo during his war trial

MEDAL & PIN
Glossary

WW II U.S. Army
Navy "E" Excellence
Production Award pin.
Page 43

"Mother's Pin"
issued in honor of
family member who
died in service
during WW II.
Page 44

Imperial Japanese
Navy war medal
Page 14

USS TENNESSEE token presented
on the day of launching
at New York Navy Yard on
April 30, 1919
Page 56

U.S. Navy
pocket watch fob
Page 52

FDR Election
campaign pin
Page 4

China War Dispatch medal
awarded to nearly all Japanese
soldiers and sailors who served
in the 1930's China Campaign.
Page 6

Home Front
pin of U.S. Navy
battleship
Page 50

Patch given to Japanese American's
serving in the 442nd Regiment.
Page 67 outside flap

World War II
Souvenir coin
Page 20

Collection of enameled
Imperial Japanese Navy medals.
Page 15, 16 & 17

Mothers' of sons in
World War II pin
Page 67

Remember Pearl Harbor pin
Front Cover

WW II U.S. Asiatic-Pacific
Campaign Medal awarded to
those who served in the Pacific
Theater from 1941 - 1945.
Page 53

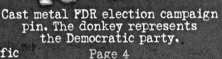

Cast metal FDR election campaign
pin. The donkey represents
the Democratic party.
Page 4

WW II "Mother's Pin."
The star represents how many sons
were serving in the military.
Page 44 & 46

Japanese Navy medal
Page 19

U.S Home Front
victory pin
Page 74

U.S. Naval Reserve
Honorable Discharge
lapel pin
Page 74

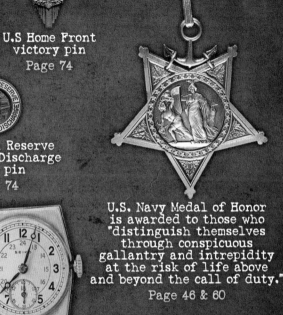

U.S. Navy Medal of Honor
is awarded to those who
"distinguish themselves
through conspicuous
gallantry and intrepidity
at the risk of life above
and beyond the call of duty."
Page 46 & 60

U.S. Navy Chief Petty
Officer collar insignia pin.
"USN" stands for Unity,
Service and Navigation.
Front Cover & Page 39

WW II U.S. Navy
"Sweetheart's Pin"
Page 48

Japanese Seikosha
(Seiko) pilot's watch
Page 24

Imperial Japanese Navy
button of Battleship Kirishima.
Page 17

The Purple Heart, the
oldest decoration in the
United States, is
awarded to those who
were wounded or lost
their lives in battle.
Page 44

Franklin Roosevelt 32nd
Presidential Commemorative coin
Page 3

"Remember Pearl
Harbor" Pin
Back Cover

Wheeler Army Airfield
7th Fighter Command patch.
Page 41

ACKNOWLEDGEMENTS

For the past twenty years, I have been writing, designing and publishing products in a variety of educational formats that narrate and illustrate the catastrophic story of the Pearl Harbor attack. I also became intrigued with the prospect of writing and designing a handmade scrapbook as if it had been created during the Pearl Harbor era. My goal was to create a book that would appeal to both a younger and older audience and present history in "bite-sized," easily readable text, yet weaving a story on each page. Working very late one night four years ago, I shared my idea with Edean Saito, Business Manager at Pacific Historic Parks "Why don't you write the book?" were her words to me as we discussed my new idea. I will never forget the look on Edean's face, nine months later, when I brought to Hawaii a presentation of the first fourteen pages as a prototype for the new scrapbook. Great care and attention to detail was taken to recreate a scrapbook that captures not only the feel, but also the integrity of the early 1940's time period. With the use of old photographs, original typefaces, newspaper articles that follow the style of the day and the use of unique and genuine artifacts from the era, we hope the reader will enjoy their adventure in a walk back into history.

I would like to thank Edean Saito, my mentor and special projects manager. I am grateful for her ongoing open mindedness and strongly believing in the concept that a Pearl Harbor scrapbook was possible. Her support, excellent editorial review and encouragement throughout the project's challenges have been significant. Her high standards and definitive feedback helped set a level of quality that I aimed for throughout this book. Thank you Edean for also taking a risk with my young publishing company when I presented my first product to you in 1991 after the 50th Anniversary of the Pearl Harbor attack.

There are other people whose collaborative efforts and talents have helped to make this book possible. It is with profound gratitude that I also acknowledge the following colleagues:

To Daniel Martinez, Chief Historian, at the World War II Valor in the Pacific National Monument at Pearl Harbor for his poignant foreword and his principled commitment to using authentic documentation which helps to illustrate this Pearl Harbor story. Daniel's insightful vision and valuable, constructive comments were crucial to the foundation of this book. I appreciate that Daniel insisted that we take no poetic license in our design, but rather, present a realistic-style scrapbook accurately recounting the history of Pearl Harbor, as well as using authentic and genuine items of the day. His generosity is greatly appreciated.

To Edward Cox, Jr., an unparalleled graphic designer, to whom I owe my deepest gratitude and admiration. It was a pleasure and a privilege to work with him. Ed worked nights, often until 2:00 a.m., deciphering my complex ideas and layouts to create some of the most visually innovative and cleverly designed elements that help make this book so unique. I interviewed Ed in the Summer of 2010. He responded by asking hundreds of intricate questions trying to understand my vision and ideas for a Pearl Harbor scrapbook. I think we talked about the ideas for this book for over a month before he actually started designing. Ed's enthusiasm for the WW II story clicked with my own passion for the Pearl Harbor story, and Ed brought amazing military facts and insight to the book that I would have never thought to incorporate or design. His innovation and drive for excellence shines on each and every page. Ed dedicated his heart and soul to this project. His humor, a consistently positive attitude, intense attention to detail and a steadfast commitment to doing "whatever it took" at any time, day or night was unfaltering in the three years we worked together on this project.

Thank you to Ernest Arroyo, Pearl Harbor historian, friend and author of the book, "PEARL HARBOR," a photographic history of "a date which will live in infamy," whose brilliant writing has brought history to life. Knowledgeable about all things Pearl Harbor, Ernest added stunning detail to the story. He contributed and enlightened me with remarkable recall on the most extraordinary facts about the Pearl Harbor story. There was never a time when I asked Ernie for his help about an aspect of the Pearl Harbor attack, or his advice on the countless pages and pages of detailed questions I submitted to him on a regular basis that he ever protested. Ernie dedicatedly responded with continuously fascinating and substantiated information. As I have told him so many times, he is a treasure. Ernie's personal collection of photographs are what make up 50% of this book. His willingness and enthusiasm to share these, as well as many other items from his personal collection was extremely generous. For all of this I am grateful.

Thank you to my husband Peter, who for four years supported my commitment to writing and designing a unique story about Pearl Harbor. His tireless patience allowed me to work well into the middle of the night, writing and researching for years, day in and day out, sequestered at my desk, often working across from him at our partner's desk. In his quiet and supportive way, he took care of everything at home to afford me the luxury of designing and writing a project about which I am so passionate. Thank you for being my constant sounding board, for your brilliant edits, your continuous help with re-writes when I was stuck and for your enthusiastic support.

Thank you to my very best fan, my daughter Peri who cheered me on from the very start at the wise old age of 9. So many nights I worked late, as she did her homework across from me, allowing me a few more hours to keep the book moving forward. Thank you for your patience when I was so deeply buried in facts and history, as well as your constant encouragement and fantastic never ending design ideas for the book. Thank you for your eagle eye in catching some important mistakes. I am so proud of you for feeling strongly about an important story in American history and for choosing to write a major school report on Pearl Harbor.

To my parents, Philip and Mariann Altfeld, my perceptive editors, sounding board and supreme cheering squad. Their abundant support helped me immeasurably in tackling a project of this size. Their unconditional belief in me helped to sustain a positive attitude during the difficult times of this job, especially when I was buried in research with no completion date in sight. I am grateful for their continued encouragement.

I would also like to express my very deep appreciation to Glenn Taubman for his brilliant editorial analysis and extensive commenting. I am appreciative of his thoughtful, critical eye and for his valuable, detailed suggestions on every draft. Thank you for your generous time to read and fine-tune the many passages throughout the numerous drafts of this project.

Bess Taubman

Japanese Fighter
Mitsubishi Type 0
"Zeke"

WHAT IF THE JAPANESE INVADED HAWAII?
WHAT WOULD HAPPEN TO HAWAII'S MONEY?

After the Japanese attack against Pearl Harbor, U.S. officials were concerned that Japan would invade and occupy Hawaii. A successful Japanese occupation could jeopardize all paper money in Hawaiian banks that in turn would deeply affect the economy of the United States, as well as in the rest of the world. To prevent this, the U.S. government recalled and burned all paper money in the Islands and reprinted $1, $5, $10 and $20 dollar bills with the name HAWAII printed on the front and the back. In the event of a Japanese occupation, the HAWAII "overprint" bills could be made worthless. It took the Treasury Department five months to overprint $65 Million Dollars worth of bills, which were ultimately recalled in 1944--ten months before Japan surrendered.

CREDITS

Photography Credits

Personal Collection of Ernest Arroyo

Official U.S. Navy Photo Collection, National Archives

Naval History and Heritage Command

Pacific Historic Parks for the use of the USS *Arizona* Memorial photos

Navsource Naval History

National Archives at College Park, College Park, MD

Naval Historical Center, Washington, D.C.

Franklin Delano Roosevelt Presidential Library

WW2 in Color

Courtesy of U.S. Army Museum of Hawaii. Photographs of Waikiki Beach and Iolani Palace surrounded in barbed wire, Page 63.

Ibiblio, National Archives

University of Hawaii Archives, Hawaii War Records Depository

University of Hawaii at Manoa Library

Archives of the Kure Maritime Museum, Japan

J. Michael Wenger

Juan Perez Collection, NPS

The Honolulu Star-Advertiser

I also wish to thank the following people and their organizations for their contribution to this project:

For the use of the internment letter from the source of: Ella C. Evanson Papers; Accession No. 2402-001, University of Washington Library, Special Collections.

For the use of World War II Japanese Internment luggage tags: Courtesy of the Matsuda Family Collection at the White River Valley Museum, Auburn, Washington; Matsuda Family Papers. Item No: 1995.0061.0001

Maryland Collection, Rare Books, and National Trust Library: Maryland Room, University of Maryland.

Sherman Seki for his enthusiastic help at the University of Hawaii Archives, Hawaii War Records Depository.

Parks Stephenson for the use of his I-16tou computer generated midget sub model.

Courtesy of The Honolulu Star-Advertiser for the use of the Honolulu newspapers from 1941.

Mike Mullins, Curator of the USS *West Virginia* Association, (www.usswestvirginia.org) for the use of treasured photographs and quotes.

William Hughes, Pearl Harbor Survivor and acting webmaster for the USS *Utah* Association, for loaning me the numerous archives relating to the USS *Utah*.

Pearl Harbor enamel badge, courtesy of William (Bill) S. Miller

Fred Harriman for proofreading the Japanese text.

Tom Freeman for the use of his paintings.

Courtesy of Hawaiian Islands Stamp and Coin, Honolulu, Hawaii for the use of the HAWAII overprint money.

Armed Forces History Division, National Museum of American History, Smithsonian Institution for the use of Edward C. Morse's Purple Heart.

Pearl Harbor Postcards

Personal Collection of Ernest Arroyo

Japanese Medals

Courtesy of: www.imperialjapanmedalsandbadges.com

Watches

Courtesy of the German Military Watch Forum

Maps

Library of Congress

Pins, Buttons and Rationing Memorabilia

Personal Collection of Bess Taubman
Personal Collection of Richard Nakasone
Personal Collection of Don Duncan

A Special Thank You...

to the many other people who helped with this project: Pearl Harbor Survivors' Families; Chris Carpenter, Jodi Wright snd Jared Stevens with Four Colour Print Group; Cary, Kim and Russ at FlyersDirect.com whose beautiful work delivered gorgeous color drafts at each stage; Ian Colbert at Fedex/Kinkos; Nikki Cox for sharing her husband Ed Cox; Weston Saito for his support; Sarah Safranski; Beverly Au; Bob Wohl; Carla Cotton for her important help in changing the order of chapters in the book; Also, deep gratitude for their caring support: David Altfeld; Shawna Erickson; Koa Watson-Japanese Warrior; Jill Feldman; Michael Feldman; Raimonde "Raimie" Bastine Harriman Manch; Melissa Caniglia; Georgette Emert; Angela Mickalide, PhD. on a chance meeting; Isaac & Elaine Taubman; Theresa Tornquist; Karen Williamson; Laurie Trotta Valenti; Dr. Arthur and Lola Weiss.

Against a pall of black oily smoke from the nearby dying Arizona, the flag of the sunken West Virginia still flies gallantly amidst the devastation.

BIBLIOGRAPHY

Adams, Henry Hitch. *1942, The Year That Doomed The Axis*. New York: David McKay Company Inc., 1967.

Adams, Henry. *Year of Deadly Peril: The Coming of the War 1939-1941*. New York: David McKay Company Inc., 1969.

Allen, Gwenfread E. *Hawaii's War Years, 1941-1945* [Prepared under the direction of the Hawaii War Records Committee of the University of Hawaii]. Honolulu, Hawaii: University of Hawaii Press, 1950.

Allen, Thomas B. *Remember Pearl Harbor: American and Japanese Survivors Tell Their Stories*. Washington, D.C.: National Geographic Society, 2001.

America In The 40's: A Sentimental Journey. Pleasantville, New York: The Readers Digest Assoc., 1998.

Arroyo, Ernest. *Pearl Harbor*. Honolulu, Hawaii: Arizona Memorial Museum Assoc., 2004.

Barr, Gary. *Pearl Harbor*. Chicago, Illinois: Heinemann Library, 2004.

Bowles, John B., and Eric C. Gross. *The Day Our World Changed: December 7, 1941: Punahou '52 Remembers Pearl Harbor*. North Liberty, Iowa: Ice Cube Press, 2004.

Bowman Reid, Constance, and Clara Marie Allen. *Slacks and Calluses: Our Summer in a Bomber Factory*. Washington, D.C.: Smithsonian Institution Press, 2004.

Brown, DeSoto, and Anne Ellett. *Hawaii Goes To War: Life In Hawaii From Pearl Harbor To Peace*. Honolulu, Hawaii: Editions Ltd., 1989.

Caren, Eric. *Pearl Harbor Extra: A Newspaper Account Of The United States' Entry Into World War II*. Edison, New Jersey: Castle Books, 2001.

Cohen, Stan. *East Wind Rain: A Pictorial History Of The Pearl Harbor Attack*. Missoula, Montana: Pictorial Histories Pub. Co., 1981.

Davis, Donald A. *Lightning Strike: The Secret Mission To Kill Admiral Yamamoto And Avenge Pearl Harbor*. New York: St. Martin's Press, 2005.

Daws, Gavan. *Shoal of Time: A History of the Hawaiian Islands*. Pbk. ed. Honolulu, Hawaii: University of Hawaii Press, 1968.

Dwiggins, Donald. *Pearl Harbor's Hero With a Hangover*. Argosy Magazine, December 1969.

Freeman, Tom, and James P. Delgado. *Pearl Harbor Recalled: New Images of the Day of Infamy*. Annapolis, Maryland: Naval Institute Press, 1991.

Gessler, Clifford. *Tropic Landfall: The Port of Honolulu*. [With plates.]. Garden City, New York: Doubleday, Doran & Co. 1942.

Hirasuna, Delphine, and Kit Hinrichs. *The Art of Gaman: Arts and Crafts from the Japanese American Internment Camps, 1942-1946*. Berkeley, California: Ten Speed Press, 2005.

Jones, Wilbur D., and Carroll Robbins Jones. *Hawaii Goes To War: The Aftermath Of Pearl Harbor*. Shippensburg, Pennsylvania: White Mane Books, 2001.

Krull, Kathleen. *V Is For Victory: America Remembers World War II*. New York: Knopf, 1995.

Lambert, John W. *The Pineapple Air Force: Pearl Harbor to Tokyo*. St. Paul, Minnesota: Phalanx Pub. Co., 1990.

Lord, Walter. *Day Of Infamy*. New York: Henry Holt & Co., 1957.

Losey, Stephen. "FDR, Al Capone's Armored Car, and Oddball Procurement Rules of the '40's." Fedline. The Beltway and Beyond. Federal Times.com. Gannett Government Media Corp., 14 July 2009. Web. Sept. 2013.

Monograph: *History of the USS Tennessee BB-48*. Navy Department; Division of Naval History, Ship's History Section.

Nicholson, Dorinda Makanaonalani Stagner. *Pearl Harbor Child: A Child's View Of Pearl Harbor--From Attack To Peace*. Honolulu, Hawaii: Arizona Memorial Museum Association, 1993.

Oppenheim, Joanne. *Dear Miss Breed: True Stories Of The Japanese American Incarceration During World War II And A Librarian Who Made A Difference*. New York: Scholastic, 2006.

Patt, Beverly, and Shula Klinger. *Best Friends Forever: A World War II Scrapbook*. New York: Marshall Cavendish Children, 2010.

Prange, Gordon W., Donald M. Goldstein, and Katherine V. Dillon. *At Dawn We Slept: The Untold Story Of Pearl Harbor*. New York: McGraw-Hill, 1981.

Richardson, James O., and George C. Dyer. *On the Treadmill to Pearl Harbor: The Memoirs of Admiral James O. Richardson*. Washington, D.C.: Department of the Navy, Naval History Division, 1973.

Rosenkrantz, Linda. *Telegram! Modern History as Told Through More than 400 Witty, Poignant, and Revealing Telegrams*. New York: Henry Holt & Co., 2003.

Seiden, Allan. *Pearl Harbor: From Fishponds To Warships: A Complete Illustrated History*. Honolulu, Hawaii: Mutual Publishing, 2001.

Simpson, MacKinnon. *Hawai'i Homefront: Life in the Islands During World War II*. Hardcover trade ed. Honolulu, Hawaii: Bess Press, 2008.

Tanaka, Shelley, and David Craig. *Attack On Pearl Harbor: The True Story Of The Day America Entered World War II*. New York: Hyperion Books For Children, 2001.

Taylor, Theodore. *Air Raid Pearl Harbor! The Story of Sunday, December 7, 1941*. San Diego, California: Harcourt Brace Jovanovich, 1991.

Time, Inc. *Pearl Harbor: America's Call to Arms*. Collector's ed. New York: Time, Inc., 2001.

Utely, Jonathon G. *An American Battleship At Peace And War: The USS Tennessee*. Lawrence, Kansas: University Press of Kansas, 1991.

Wallin, Vice Admiral Homer N. *Pearl Harbor: Why, How, Fleet Salvage and Final Appraisal*. Washington D.C.: U.S. Government Printing Office, 1968.

My own photo of
Pearl Harbor

Notes from my trip
to Pearl Harbor